CAPONE OF CANNABIS

Capone Of Cannabis

Ryan Richmond

ZS GROUP
PUBLISHERS

For my children—so one day you'll understand why
prison took me 420 miles from you and your mom, and
how hard I worked to come back home.

Contents

1

Early Days in the Green Rush

Before I was a criminal. Before the headlines, the mugshots, the federal indictment, the Supreme Court and the prison ID number. Before the raids that ripped the doors off my shops and my life—I was just another white guy in a suit. Leasing office space to doctors and lawyers, spending my days in conference rooms and on the phone with clients, chasing commission checks and managing others. At night, I slept like a baby.

It was fine work, respectable work, but it felt like I was always helping other people build their dream, build something new, while I just moved paper from one desk to another. I wasn't exactly reinventing the wheel.

Then, one cold afternoon in late 2009, my phone rang.

"Do you know any buildings in Royal Oak? We're looking to open a marijuana dispensary."

Up to that point, my experience with marijuana was limited to high school, college, and the occasional weekend toke. I knew it well enough to recognize it—but not nearly well enough to think I was qualified to sell it.

I didn't catch his name at first — Nick, I'd later learn. He didn't sound like the kind of guy you'd picture when someone said "pot dealer." He was quick, clear, and confident. His voice had energy, like

a man who had already visualized what he wanted and was just looking for someone to help him make it real.

His number had a Colorado area code — and back then, that mattered. Michigan had just passed its medical marijuana law that legalized the medical use of cannabis, but Colorado was a couple of years
ahead, figuring out what this new industry could look like.

Nick and his partners were born and raised in Michigan and became early pioneers, now veterans, of Colorado's cannabis experiment. They were bringing that knowledge back home.

I didn't know it yet, but that phone call would change the rest of
my life.

* * *

Nick's call lit me up — not just because there was money in it, but
because it was new. Entire industries don't crawl out of the shadows
every day. It felt like standing on the edge of a new frontier, like strik-
ing gold in the 1840s — only this gold came with lawyers, cops, and
the press watching your every move.

I hung up and stared at the phone. The office felt louder than
usual—the HVAC, the street, my own heartbeat. Motivational quotes
stared back at me from cheap frames on the wall, and my desk was a
mess of maps, lease comps, and market spreadsheets. Normally, a call
meant another tour, another negotiation, another commission check.
But this one was different. There were no existing dispensaries to
lease, no comps to anchor a rate per square foot—no blueprint at all.
I'd be inventing it as I went. For the first time in a long time, I wasn't
just "working a deal." I was stepping into a brand-new market. And I
was excited.

Michigan voters had just done something extraordinary. After
years of debate and moral panic, they passed a statewide medical marijuana law—and not by a slim margin. Nearly two-thirds of voters
said yes to Proposal 1, which legalized the use of medical marijuana
for "qualifying patients"—that is, individuals with certain debilitating

medical conditions. It was a landslide victory that cut across party lines, generations, economics and geography.

But if you were anywhere near a courtroom, a prosecutor's office, or a police union hall in 2009, you could feel the anger humming through the system. This wasn't just another ballot measure. This was a direct challenge to decades of "Just Say No" orthodoxy, D.A.R.E. programs, and the steady revenue of the drug war.

The most visible face of that resistance was Bill Schuette—former judge, former congressman, and soon-to-be Michigan Attorney General. Schuette had lent his name to a PAC called Citizens Protecting Michigan's Kids, better known as No Pot Shops. Their website—bluntly titled NoPotShops.com—became ground zero for the campaign against Proposal 1. Schuette was cringey in that uniquely politicalway: self-satisfied, camera-trained, the type of man who mistakes attention for approval and the spotlight for proof of virtue.

His message was simple: if Michigan allowed this, the state would turn into "the next California," where medical marijuana had been legalized under the 1996 Compassionate Use Act. He painted Michigan like a Reefer Madness rerun—dispensaries on every corner, cops drowning in a tide of pothead zombies, stoned kids loitering in school parking lots, and highways packed with high drivers.

"There is not a single paragraph, sentence or word within Proposal 1 that prohibits pot shops from opening in Michigan, just like they did in California." said Schuette.

He also insisted medical marijuana wasn't about medicine at all — it was a Trojan horse for full-blown legalization.

The No Pot Shops website listed the following warnings, each one sounding like the end of civilization:

...that a flaw in Proposal 1 might lead to a flood of lawsuits over things such as whether doctors and hospitals must allow patients to smoke marijuana in a doctor's office or hospital room.

...that when a similar law passed in California, hundreds of marijuana smoking clubs opened in neighborhood strip malls all over the state, and there are now more marijuana clubs in one metropolitan area than there are Starbucks coffee shops.

…that the language of the proposal requires a costly new Lansing bureaucracy to license marijuana users, and will result in vast new regulatory expenses.

…that Proposal 1 could lead to a dangerous increase in the number of people driving under the influence of marijuana.

…that a deliberate loophole in Proposal 1 allows anyone arrested on any offense involving marijuana to offer a "medical" defense in court.

After Michigan's medical marijuana law passed, Mr. Schuette was soon elected the state's Attorney General—and with that power, he suddenly read the law very differently. He now insisted the Michigan Medical Marihuana Act never allowed for dispensaries and then led the charge to shut them all down.

And this was the world I was about to step into.

2

Early Life

When people ask where I grew up and I say "Clarkston," I can see the assumption land immediately. They picture privilege—the boutique, the lake-life, the polished version of Clarkston people know today.

The truth couldn't be further from it.

My grandparents hauled eight kids out of rural Appalachian Pennsylvania and they arrived in a Clarkston that is unrecognizable by even the oldest Clarkstonians. I was raised on the same dirt road, a few houses from the family homestead, watching suburban sprawl creep in like ivy. New subdivisions, new money, new schools.

I loved my family. I loved the blue-collar neighbors I grew up around. But at school I saw the other side of town up close—kids with new shoes, name-brand clothes, two-parent homes that felt sturdy, like they'd been built to last. I didn't feel comfortable in the hallways of the school I attended, but I felt even less comfortable at home. Like I was always in the wrong place, no matter which place I was in.

The only thing I knew for sure was that I needed out.

I did all the things kids did before the internet. I rode bikes until nightfall set in, built forts out of scrap wood, and lived on ballfields. But something in me was different. I wanted more—something I didn't learn at home or from the neighborhood. I wanted a challenge. I wanted to see how far I could push myself.

As early as I can remember, I worked. I had a paper route at ten, mowed lawns at twelve, umpired little league games, and by middle school I'd built what I can only describe as a baseball card empire. It started with Shark Tank negotiations on the school bus—me and a couple neighborhood kids huddled over a binder, arguing like tiny executives over a Ken Griffey Jr. rookie. But I wasn't satisfied trading with kids who only knew what their older brothers told them. I wanted the adult circuit.

I demanded my parents take me to card shows so I could trade with the sharks—grown men who could smell a good deal the way dogs smell bacon. I watched. I learned. I figured out what made people say yes, what made them hesitate, and what made them hand over value without realizing it.

Then I discovered autographs. I started writing letters to athletes, asking for signatures like I was running a miniature PR firm out of my bedroom. When a few actually came back, I treated it like proof of concept. I organized everything I'd learned into a little manual—How to Get Autographs From Home—and I ran classifieds in sports-card magazines selling my "system" to other collectors.

The ad read: RUSH $10 CASH to Ryan Richmond—right next to my mother's home address.

The autograph address list was typed up on a neighbor's computer and printed out. I was running a mail-order business. Money started flowing in. And as long as I got to the mailbox before Mom got home from work, no one would be the wiser. If checks were sent, they got thrown away. I was too young for a bank account. But the cash? The cash was all mine.

It worked… until the day it didn't.

Mom had a rare day off. She checked the mailbox that day before me.

By then my little operation had expanded, and the revenue was parlayed into an ad that had made its way into the National Enquirer.

The big leagues. I can still see her standing there, envelope in one hand, the cash in the other, face lit up with disbelief and anger.

"You put our home address in the paper," she said. "What the hell are you doing?"

At the time, she was livid—and who could blame her? But I'd learn later there was pride buried underneath it.

My teenage years turned into reselling whatever I could get my hands on. And eventually, like a lot of kids with too much ambition and not enough runway, I drifted into dime bags of weed at lunch—scoring from older guys in the neighborhood and flipping to whoever had lunch money to spend.

But here's what matters: I never wanted to be like the guys I bought weed from. I wasn't trying to become a neighborhood legend. I was looking for a way out.

Because when you keep seeing the same twenty-something-year-old pot dealer showing up at high school field parties—like time never moved forward for him—you start to understand what staying can look like.

I didn't want that.

There wasn't pressure from either parent to go to college, even though my grades were solid. Nobody spread applications across the kitchen table. It just wasn't talked about—maybe because there wasn't any money set aside to pay for it.

One day, cutting class—maybe to smoke or sell a joint—I got pinched by a teacher.

"What are you doing?" she said. "Aren't you supposed to be in class?"

As I stood there, annoyed and caught, my eyes and alibi drifted to a poster on the wall: MEET THE ARMY RECRUITER.

The teacher read from the poster that the recruiter wouldn't be in until later that week. But the idea had already started forming in my head, piece by piece. The Army wasn't just a job—it was a path. A way out.

It was also something that would make my parents proud of me. Everybody respects a soldier.

I wasn't old enough to enlist, which meant I'd need a parent there to sign in front of the recruiter. And as that day got closer—and the Iraq war headlines and Bosnia footage replayed in my mind—I started second-guessing myself.

I remember thinking: You know… maybe the Air Force could be a better option.

After graduating high school and months into my new Air Force career, I started second-guessing everything.

Not because I was scared. Because I was offended—by the structure, by the sameness, by the idea that I was supposed to shrink myself into a system that rewarded obedience over imagination. I told myself I was better than this. Smarter than my superiors. Smarter than the machine that ran on yes-sir and no-sir.

I wasn't built for marching in straight lines.

So I did what I always do when I feel trapped: I looked for a way out that didn't involve breaking down. I didn't want to fake insanity. I wanted a clean exit. A legitimate one.

I took the night shift so I could go to community college during the day. I lived on caffeine and stubbornness, grinding through homework while the base slept. And in my off hours, I searched the regulations like they were a map that might offer a solution.

That's when I found it—buried deep in the manuals, the kind of program most people never hear about and even fewer dare to try. A provision that would let you separate after two years of active duty if you agreed to serve six more years part time in the Reserves or National Guard.

In the military, rule number one is to obey the chain of command. Rule number two is don't make your chain of command look bad. My paperwork went up the line and then vanished into silence. No acknowledgment. No decision. Just dormancy—the bureaucratic version of "no."

So I went on the offensive.

I started working my way upward, appealing to officers—the ones in the military with degrees, the ones trained to speak in diplomacy. I framed it carefully: I was trying to get an education. I was trying to improve myself. I wanted to become an officer like them. The work schedule was making it difficult. My work ethic and supervisor reports were excellent. I didn't complain; I presented a problem with a solution already attached.

Eventually I went way higher than I was supposed to. I confronted the base colonel—the number two in charge.

It was a gamble. But I believed I knew how to sell myself without upsetting the balance. I knew how to ask for what I wanted without making anyone feel disrespected. I didn't accuse the system—I praised it. I didn't demand—I proposed. I made it sound like approving me wasn't bending the rules. It was the rules working exactly as they were intended.

And just like that, my request was approved.

* * *

My mother was beautiful. That wasn't always easy as a kid, especially when friends would constantly remind me, 'Dude, your mom is hot'. But behind her smile was constant pain. She battled Lupus for most of her life, a disease that eventually took her two days shy of my 25th birthday.

Part of the reason I liked the medical marijuana space was rooted in a memory from college. I was in the National Guard at the time—one weekend a month—and I'd stay with mom at her apartment during those weekends. One Friday night I came home to find her crying on the couch.

"Mom, what's wrong?" I asked.

She was embarrassed to tell me but explained that her once-a-month steroid injection never lasted the full 30 days. She was supplementing with cannabis to manage the pain, but now she was out.

Her dealer — some guy from her neighborhood — had his phone disconnected. Probably busted. Maybe by the same task force and Sheriff that would end up chasing after me.

"I'll get you some," I told her.

After Guard duty the next day, I drove back to the old neighborhood — I knew where to go. I bought her a bag, and brought it home. She was grateful, but later admitted, "It's not as good as what I usually get."

* * *

After studying business in college, I wanted a job people respected. Not just money—status. I wanted other people to look at me and nod like I belonged. I wanted to be cool, or at least wear the uniform of cool.

Hollywood had already done the sales pitch: the stockbroker as kingmaker, exciting, and genius in a suit. So I decided that sounded good.

I interned at the stock brokerage firm of Dean Witter. The office was chaos—phones ringing, paperwork stacked like a collapsing skyline, and a complete lack of proper management or training. After a couple of weeks I moved on to another firm. At the time it felt like a simple career adjustment.

It was the second best decision I ever made.

At the other firm, the rule was clear: new brokers had to spend six weeks in the New York headquarters. That requirement would have placed me inside the World Trade Center—right when the planes hit on 9/11.

After that, I threw myself into work. I liked being a financial planner. Not the glossy part—suits and douchebaggery—but the real part: helping ordinary people win. My family and friends' parents were mostly blue-collar. They knew hard work, they knew bills, and they knew the comfort of paying off a house and parking money in CDs.

Investing felt like a foreign language to them. I became their translator.

The market was bullish, and the timing made me look like a genius. I helped increase the net worth of people who'd never seen their accounts grow like that. For a while, I was the family hero—the guy who could turn General Motors overtime money into something that actually moved.

And then I got out before it crashed.

I sold my book of business, took the capital and momentum, flipped a few houses, and found my way into the real estate business—an industry that, at the time, felt like a cheat code.

Around then, I met Sarah.

Sarah stood by me as I transitioned from financial sales into commercial real estate, where I met one of Detroit's sharpest business minds—and before I was thirty, the two of us started our own firm. I was an eternal student of anything that was new. I taught myself to code at night—HTML, basic scripting—anything I could use to make a boring, antiquated industry move faster. I merged the old-world handshake business of commercial real estate with the new-world reality of online marketing.

Leads started rolling in. Then something else happened: sixty-year-old brokers—men who'd been in the game longer than I'd been alive—started calling me, wanting to work with me, asking how I was doing it. They weren't used to chasing business online. That was all I knew.

And that marketing—my little engine—eventually caught the attention of Nick and the first wave of would-be dispensary owners.

3

My First Cannabis Investment

Nick didn't know Michigan politics or real estate — but I did. I knew the landlords, the zoning boards, the small-town politics. I knew how to ask for something that didn't exist. Or so I thought.

What none of us realized was how quickly the opposition would regroup after losing at the ballot box. "No Pot Shops" didn't vanish after Election Day — they just changed strategies.

My first job for Nick's crew was simple: find a building for them and negotiate the lease on their behalf.

Finding one was like trying to lease space for a strip club next to an elementary school. Landlords were skittish, other real estate brokers sceptical, and cities started passing zoning moratoriums like they were handing out candy—90 days here, 180 there, "temporary" bans that were somehow renewed every meeting. I'd sit through council sessions under buzzing fluorescent lights, watching ancient residents and decaying politicians take turns at the mic to predict the storefront would turn their cul-de-sacs into Fallujah.

They'd clutch pearls over "criminal elements," warn of reefer madness traffic jams, ask if "the smell" could seep through drywall and rot the minds of children. A pastor would cite scripture. A realtor would cite "property values." A self-appointed neighborhood historian would talk about the time the roller rink closed and "everything went downhill," like a dispensary was the four horsemen on a POS system.

Some meetings got tense. You could feel the room tighten. One councilman wagged a pen at me and said, "We don't need drug dealers in lab coats." Another asked if we could promise "only medical marijuana, not the addictive kind."

Landlords weren't just spooked—they were insured. Their carriers sent letters warning that leasing to a cannabis business could void coverage. Banks slid collateral clauses across the table, hinting that a friendly visit from the feds might sweep up the building in forfeiture Even the brave owners who liked us would lower their voices and say, "I want to do this, but my investors will kill me." I couldn't blame them. Fear had better lobbyists than we did.

So I learned the choreography. I brought graphs, crime stats from legal states, made friends with a security contractor in a tie, a retired nurse with a calm voice, and a veteran on a cane who could join me at council meetings if I needed. I pre-met with planning staff, rewrote conditions in their language, and offered to fund crosswalks, planters, trash cans—anything that would make the Colorado crew look like the most boring, responsible neighbors on earth.

Every call, every tour, every council session ended the same way: "Not here." Not because of facts. Because fear felt safer to endorse than change.

After months of chasing dead ends, I told Nick that I was out. Too much work. Too much risk to my real estate business and my employees. The juice wasn't worth the squeeze.

They came back — not with another building, but with a proposition: stop being just our broker and become our partner.

I hesitated. I had a career. A wife and two cats. But the truth was, I was already in. The disruption was too exciting to ignore. The law was on our side — or so I thought. A few days later, I countered their terms. They accepted right away.

My former boss owned a lot of real estate in Metro Detroit including the largest commercial property portfolio in Ferndale — a progressive city known for its LGBTQ community and open politics. If any city would give us a shot, it was Ferndale. And if he was going to rent a building for the purpose of selling a drug he didn't understand, it would be to me—not a couple of strangers from Colorado. That's how the chain of command works in the real world.

I approached him about leasing one of his properties, then got to work winning over the city council and mayor. Those meetings were a little tense but productive — I explained how the operation would work, how we'd keep the community safe, and how we'd be different from the "pot shop" image that haunted people's imaginations.

The city signed off. My landlord signed off. I put up most of the money. And the Colorado crew did what they knew best—locking in supply lines, dialing in the infrastructure, and handling the buildout.

A couple of months later, the Detroit Free Press ran a front-page headline: Medical Marijuana For Sale In Ferndale

Just like that, we were live.

* * *

We named the dispensary Clinical Relief. Clean. Professional. No neon pot leaves, no Bob Marley posters, no stoner branding. That was my condition to my new partners. We became Michigan's first licensed medical marijuana dispensary.

For Nick, it became a family business—one that finally let them spend more time together after his long absence in Colorado. His brother Tony, a tight-muscled gym rat, had quit a lucrative job to manage the shop. Their parents, both in their late sixties, worked the front desk part-time and became beloved fixtures. One of my friends and two close family friends of Nick joined as budtenders — including the daughter of Detroit Tigers legend Mickey Lolich.

Opening day didn't feel like we were launching a store.

It felt like we were cutting the ribbon on a movement—one I'd backed personally, financially, and deliberately.

The dispensary, a converted loft office space, was bright, spotless, humming with nervous energy. Think Starbucks meets Chipotle meets CVS. Neutral tones, exposed ductwork, polished concrete floors. If you didn't look too hard, you might've mistaken it for a trendy cafe—until the scent of weed hit you.

The shelves were stocked. The front desk was dialed in. Our crew suited up in crisp white lab coats and name badges—part pharmacist, part bad ass. The phone system and website had been tested and then retested again. And back then—before the banks got cold feet and yanked their support from the entire cannabis industry—our credit card terminals sat ready, hungry for plastic. Every detail was intentional. Every intake form, every shelf layout, every patient interaction had been mapped out like a battle plan.

We weren't just opening a store—we were setting a standard. We wanted to define what it meant to buy cannabis in Michigan: professional, safe, and legitimate. And for me, it wasn't only about making money—it was about helping people like my mom, the ones who needed relief and deserved dignity.

This was more than a grand opening.

It was a middle finger to decades of prohibition. It marked the beginning of the end of handoffs in parking lots, the awkward wait in some guy's smoky living room while he finished a video game before weighing out your sack. No more shady apartments, no more awkward small talk, no more finding out that your dealer had his phone disconnected.

Patients came in cautiously at first, some walking with canes, others peeking around the door like they still couldn't believe it was legal. Their shoulders dropped when they realized they weren't about to be arrested. They asked questions, smelled the Mason jars filled with buds, and left with medicine — and relief.

Nick's mom ran the front desk, greeting every patient like they were an old neighbor. Tony kept the back running like a machine: inventory tight, security tighter, and not a gram out of place. Nick was the face—the palm presser, the handshake king.

And then there was me. The so-called "silent" partner. I showed up to watch the excitement, soak in the energy, offer some feedback—and then rush back to my day job, still trying to juggle both lives. I wasn't involved in the day-to-day, but I was always watching, always thinking, always building the next move in my head.

Within a week of opening, the media descended. The Free Press ran another story, TV crews showed up, and our phones rang nonstop. Patients drove in from every corner of Michigan, lining up outside or crowding the lobby just to get their medicine.

Customers at the counters would eventually tell us about being approached by rival dealers—less organized, less reputable—trying to poach them while they parked their cars or waited in the lobby to be served.

"I can sell you better stuff for less money."

It didn't stop there. That pattern followed me the entire time I was in the cannabis business. They didn't risk a dollar to open the doors. They didn't sign the leases, front the payroll, or put their necks on the line. They just hovered at the edges and fed off the work and investment we'd already made.

And it pissed me off.

Local police even stopped by — not to raid us or arrest the poachers, but to talk about security. City council members and neighboring politicians toured the shop, asked questions, nodded in approval. For a moment, it felt like we had built something everyone could agree on.

Patients lingered after purchases, sharing stories of cancer treatments, MS pain, PTSD nightmares. Sometimes they cried. Sometimes we did too.

After clocking out of my day job, some nights I'd swing by the shop—usually right before they locked the front doors. The lights were dimmed, the noise of the day replaced by that late-night stillness you only notice when a place has finally exhaled. The edibles fridge hummed in the corner—soft and steady A couple of the crew would still be there, counting down the register or restocking shelves for tomorrow like it was any other business.

I'd lean against the counter, loosen my tie, and just take it in.

Because it wasn't any other business. Not to me.

My two worlds were colliding in that quiet hour: the polished, buttoned-up commercial real estate grind I did in daylight, and this after-hours frontier where we sold something that actually helped people. I could feel both identities on my shoulders—the professional who spoke in square feet and cap rates, and the guy who'd built a shop that smelled of skunk and possibility.

And for once, it didn't feel like just another deal. I remember thinking, This is what it feels like to build something that matters. Like I was reinventing the wheel.

Then we'd gather in the back, surrounded by open ledgers, half-filled jars, and the scent of the day still lingering in the air. A joint would get passed around, the smoke curling toward the cracked open door. These weren't just end-of-day wind-downs — they were the early blueprints of something bigger. Strategy meetings disguised as smoke sessions, full of belief and ambition.

Clinical Relief gave all of us purpose. For the elder Agros, retirement became exciting again. For Tony, work became personal.

For a little while, we were unstoppable.

We were Michigan's first licensed medical marijuana dispensary. We were helping the sick. We were open. We were proud.

And for a brief, shining moment, it felt like we were winning.

4

The Family Burial Plot

I've always known my immediate family—my uncles and aunts, their kids, the tight circle you can point to at weddings and funerals and say, that's us.

Anything beyond that was a blank space. A locked drawer. A part of the Richmond story nobody opened, nobody aired out, like talking about it might invite it back in.

When the Richmonds came down out of the Pennsylvania hills, they didn't just move—they vanished. They left everything behind. Not even a single story packed in the suitcase. No "back home" legends. No funny uncle with the mule. No old-world recipe. Nothing. Just a hard stop, like somebody slammed a door and threw the key into the Ohio river as they crossed.

Why Grandpa and Grandma left still sits there like an unanswered knock.

Most people from those hills traveled the thing they call the Hillbilly Highway—the Appalachia spilling into Detroit, chasing factory paychecks and union protection. A road paved with shift whistles and overtime and hope that came wrapped in metal. But Grandpa didn't land one of those jobs.

It always felt like he wasn't chasing work. It felt like he was running.

Running from what, he never said. He carried it like contraband—kept it hidden, kept it close, and took it straight to the ground

18

with him. Buried it in the Michigan Richmond family plot like a final act of control. He was the first one laid there. The others would arrive over the years, one by one, as if the soil itself was collecting them.

And Grandma—Grandma was left behind in the living world with the part nobody romanticizes: poverty, scars from abuse, exhaustion and eight kids packed into a two-bedroom house that was too small for their bodies and way too small for their fear. Those kids didn't "grow up" so much as they escaped. The moment they were old enough, every single one left—married or clocking in at General Motors, grabbing whatever stability they could get their hands on.

Sometimes I can't decide which child had it the worst.

The older ones that had lived through the full force of grandpa—his moods, his hands, his drinking, the unpredictable weather of a man who could turn the whole house into a storm.

Or my father—the youngest—who only had just enough time to form memories before his dad was gone. Just enough to feel the shadow, but not enough to understand its shape. The kind of half-memory that doesn't give you answers, only questions. As his siblings left my father was left holding the absence. A kid trying to make sense of a father who was both monster and missing person.

* * *

If Dad grew up in squalor, then Mom—by comparison—was a Rockefeller.

In the quiet luxury of two suburban parents with high school degrees, and extended family close enough to drop by and trade family stories. More like the parents of the kids I went to school with than the parents I grew up with. Two people who weren't at war every night. A house where the adults might be tired—but they weren't dangerous.

But she wasn't exactly safe in the way people imagine when they hear "good family." She wasn't neglected the way Dad was, not in the obvious, cinematic ways. She wasn't abandoned by fists or liquor.

She was abandoned by distance.

By years of separation from siblings who were already halfway out the door by the time she came online. By the strange loneliness of being the "surprise baby"—the last one—showing up when Grandma and Grandpa were older, slower, spent.

Mom was a hippie—at least in the way the word really means when it's not a costume.

She was finding her own path—not asking permission, not asking for direction from parents who had already changed titles from parent to grandparent five years before she graduated high school.

That path found its way to my dad before she turned twenty.

A couple months later, I showed up—less a plan than a collision—and somehow I became the glue. The reason. The excuse that made two drifting people stop to build something that looked like a life.

I'm telling you all of this about my grandparents—my parents, their short courtship—not as fact, because I was raised on silence. These are just observations from a curious kid.

No stories about their lives were shared at the dinner table or during holidays. No stories about their parents or grandparents. No origin myths. No romance you could hold up like a lantern and say, this is where we came from.

Just fragments. A few facts—from that one slightly less reserved aunt.

And as a kid, you can feel that. You can feel the missing chapters like a draft under the door. You can hear it in the way questions land and nobody picks them up. You learn, early, that some subjects make grown-ups stare at the table like it's got the answer.

Silence isn't neutral. It teaches you what's allowed. It teaches you what hurts. It teaches you what people are trying to bury—even if you don't know exactly what it is yet.

So I grew up with questions—and the early knowledge that I'd never get the real answers. Not because I wasn't curious enough, but because the people who held them didn't know them... or wouldn't.

And when you realize that, you start doing the only thing you can do.

You start digging.

If I was going to get an oral history, I'd have to build it myself—from paper.

So I got to work. I paid for a premium subscription to Ancestry, that online database built for people like me: the ones handed silence and told to call it "privacy." The ones trying to turn blank space into a timeline.

But it was something. Names. Dates. Census lines. Draft cards. Death certificates. Cold ink that could still point a finger in the right direction.

At least on paper, I could start making sense of where I came from. And what I learned would make absolute sense to my life and what it meant to be a Richmond.

5

Wedding Vows and Business Deals

Gary wasn't just my cousin — he was basically my older brother. We grew up a few blocks apart and spent a lot of our time together. Or as much as Gary would allow. He had two older sisters, so I ended up filling the role of kid brother: tagging along, learning about girls, and taking my fair share of abuse just for being the younger one. But in a working class neighborhood like ours — where getting pushed around was the norm — having someone like Gary helped. He taught me how to handle myself. And when things got real bad, I knew he'd be there.

We shared more than just geography. Gary's mother and my father — siblings — were both alcoholics, haunted by the same demons that plagued their own father, who died before either of us were born.

We both knew what the combo of parental neglect, poverty, and—eventually—alcohol does to a person. We'd watched it happen in real time to our parents and its effects. We understood that neither of them was ever really present, not in the way a kid needs. Maybe they didn't really know how to be parents. Maybe no one ever showed them.

But when you're a kid, you don't have that kind of vernacular. You don't get to diagnose the room. You just feel the absence and assume it's normal. You don't examine it like the men we are now—you just grow up inside it.

Whether by nature or nurture, our lives ran parallel. And much later on in our life, we'd both come to realize that cannabis was a better choice than the chaos and cruelty we experienced from alcoholic parents. Weed didn't yell. It didn't shame. It didn't leave scars.

That didn't mean we avoided alcohol—we partied, we lived it up. Gary followed me to Central Michigan University and we joined the same fraternity, on a campus that, just five years earlier, Playboy had ranked among its top 40 party schools.

So when Gary announced he was getting married in Las Vegas, one month after I'd opened Clinical Relief, my wife and I booked our flight and hotel room. Vegas was the perfect setting for celebration and excess — especially for frat brothers who invented 'having a good time'. The wedding guest list was a reunion of family and Gary's football crew from high school: big personalities, even bigger drinks. The entire weekend was perfect.

Over that weekend, the conversation turned to my involvement in the medical marijuana business. At the time, the press was buzzing about it — and about me. You couldn't flip through a newspaper without reading something about weed in Michigan.

I was caught off guard when two of Gary's friends showed real interest in what I was doing. One of them was Jeremy — though we all called him Doty — an Oakland County cop with close ties to my family. During the wedding party, in one of Caesar's private event rooms, he reached out—trying to land a job for his fiancée. Doty wasn't just a friend; he was an extended family member. Anyone from the Midwest knows that being part of the annual deer camp earns you a permanent place at the table — sometimes even more than blood. And, in our younger years, when the crew went barhopping, Doty wasn't just along for the ride — he was the unofficial, designated drunk driver.

The other was Jake—recently laid off, MBA on his résumé, and full of questions. I remembered him from high school, but until that weekend I couldn't recall a single conversation we'd ever had.

Both were classic meathead drinkers — hard-partiers, no-cannabis types. And yet here they were, curious about the pot biz. What did they know about weed? Probably nothing. But I humored the conversation, promising we'd revisit the idea when we were sober and back in Michigan.

To my surprise, Jake followed up.

Jake didn't fit the usual mold. He didn't smoke weed. That made him somewhat more productive and organized to me than the Colorado boys. His business background and education were solid and he was good at numbers and spreadsheets where I was good at running my mouth. So we decided — rather, I demanded — to bring him on as a partner.

But I'd learned my lessons from previous business ventures with business partners who had great ideas but lacked financial investment chaining them to the venture. I wasn't taking on anyone who didn't have skin in the game. Jake and his wife agreed to fund their end of the partnership by borrowing from his old employer's 401(k). That cash became some of the seed money for our second dispensary, this time in Lansing.

We called it Clinical Relief of Lansing — a continuation of the brand we'd started. This wasn't just about helping the sick anymore. We were building something bigger. We were planning to own the entire Michigan medical cannabis market.

I quickly got to work selecting other markets to open up shop while maintaining my day job as the owner of a commercial real estate firm. I was still navigating zoning meetings, lease

proposals, and building codes by day — but at night, we strategized around strains, margins, and security plans. My two worlds ran in parallel, each more demanding than the other.

Doty's fiancée did end up getting a job — working directly under Jake after he arranged for it. It wasn't just a favor or an attempt to gain legitimacy by hiring a cop's soon to be wife. She was competent, and the hire made sense at the time. But it wasn't long after she was hired on that Doty made a curious career move of his own: Gary shared with me that he joined the Oakland County Narcotics Enforcement Team or NET for short.

NET was headed by Sheriff Bouchard—a general in the No Pot Shops army. A staunch opponent of the change voters had decided on, and of the businesses the Colorado boys and I were building.

At the time, I didn't think much about Doty working there. Why would he want to hurt Jake or me—and more importantly, his fiancée?

Meanwhile, Jake became the quiet force behind our expansion. Calculated. Steady. And reliable. He was the kind of guy who showed up early and kept his receipts. I trusted him. He was allowed into every layer of the operation — from vendor negotiations to staff meetings to financials. Unlike the Colorado crew, he wasn't getting high on the job — and it helped his performance.

Vegas — the networking capital of the world — felt less like a wedding and more like an industry event. But what I didn't know then — couldn't have known — was that the same people toasting my success and asking favors would help destroy it.

6

The First Raid

Less than three months after Clinical Relief opened its doors—something the state had never seen before—the war on medical cannabis came to Ferndale.

I was leaving work, still in my suit, still carrying the day's polite conversations like they mattered, when I decided to swing by the shop. Just a quick check-in—say hi to the crew, walk the floor, make sure everything looked right. Check on my new baby.

That's what it felt like back then: a newborn business, just learning to breathe.

And then I crossed north of Eight Mile.

Armored vehicles. Flashing lights. A literal tank parked out front like we were an enemy position. Police in gear moving with that rehearsed certainty. And media vans—already there, already setting up, cameras angled for the shot that would tell the public what to think before anyone knew the facts.

My hands tightened on the wheel. My mouth went dry. For a second my mind tried to negotiate—Maybe it's next door. Maybe it's a drill. Maybe I'm reading it wrong.

But I wasn't.

I didn't stop. I kept driving, suit and tie and Cadillac rolling past my own storefront like I was a stranger.

I drove on, heart banging, eyes flicking to the mirror like I expected them to turn and follow.

But the raid had already spread

When I got home, I found my life in ruins. Agents had already broken in, tearing through everything. My indoor cats ran wild and terrified. Drawers dumped. Closets ripped open. My home, and my sense of safety, violated beyond recognition.

I didn't dare go in. I parked a street over and watched the mayhem unfold—like the nosy neighbors standing in their front yards, except I was hunched behind my windshield, trying to look invisible in my own car. Then I drove to the nearest ATM, pulled some cash, and checked into a room under a fictitious name on the 70th floor of the Renaissance Center in downtown Detroit. I needed height. I needed distance. I needed to see the threat before it arrived again.

My wife was in Atlanta on a business trip. For a few days, it was just me and the mess I'd made. I waited until she came home to tell her what had happened.

Nick's family wasn't as lucky. His brother's house was also raided. Their wives and young children faced masked men with assault rifles and no mercy. Bedrooms destroyed. Piggy banks seized. Their homes weren't just searched — they were desecrated. Whatever innocence was left in those houses died that night.

I would later learn that even our patients didn't escape the trauma. One woman — 68 years old and a breast cancer survivor — was tackled to the floor while trying to explain she was just there to pick up her medicine. Another, a military veteran with a PTSD card, was held at gunpoint, triggering the very kind of episode she used cannabis to manage.

Nick's mother and brother. Mickey Lolich's daughter. My friend Ryan and a wheelchair-bound grandma with multiple sclerosis were also treated like violent criminals for the "crime" of participating in a voter-approved medical cannabis program.

The officers didn't blink. No pause. No apology. Just boots on necks and guns in faces—because that's what the badge and the narrative demanded.

I was pissed off—and caught completely off guard. And to keep the Sheriff from owning the narrative he wanted to feed the public, I ran to the press and got our side out as quickly as I could.

Richmond said police took a total of about 6 ounces of marijuana from the clinic and raided his Royal Oak house where they took TVs, computers, documents and a couple of hunting rifles that were in the basement. There was no marijuana at his house, he said. "I believe we are a test case for law enforcement and prosecutors to challenge this new law" Richmond said. "We only sell to licensed patients. But we are seeing the reality of how the world works." - Oakland Press

The raid occurred on a Friday evening — the sweet spot for raids, when 90% of dispensary busts seemed to go down, always after 6 p.m. That's when shops were flush with cash, inventory was stocked for the weekend, and credit card terminals were loaded from a week's worth of patient sales. It also happened to be when government overtime kicked in.

Two days after Ferndale city leaders lifted a moratorium on any new medical marijuana businesses and amended local zoning ordinances to allow them in certain sections of the city., the No Pot Shop's crew along with the Oakland County Narcotics Team — Doty's new crew — made their move.

A full-blown tactical assault, led by anti-cannabis hardliner and resident douchebag, the county Sheriff. Rifles up. Faces masked. Patients and staff thrown to the ground like they were knocking over a cartel warehouse — not a voter-approved medical dispensary.

A couple days after the raid, I found myself back inside the dispensary—now dark and shuttered—with Nick and our friend Stick, a popular radio DJ. We stood in the silence trying to figure out how to pick up the pieces, like men staring at a wrecked car and arguing whether it could still drive.

"What do we do next?"

"Do we reopen?"

"What lawyers do we hire?"

Then Nick's cell phone rang. Nick answered. Stick and I looked up. Nick was already sobbing. "My dad is dead." Nick's father, Sal, who worked part-time at the shop, retired from the auto industry and coaching football for the city of Lake Orion, had suffered a massive heart attack just days after the brutal raids on his wife, his children, and his grandchildren. His whole family.

Stick and I looked at each other in shock, not knowing what to say. So we said nothing. We just hugged Nick—the only language that felt appropriate.

Sal had spent his life on the sidelines, teaching boys to stand up straight and finish what they started. At his funeral the church overflowed—friends, family, and hundreds of former high-school players who still called him coach.

I called him a friend. And in that moment I felt responsible for bringing this venture—this dispensary—to life. I know Sal would've told me, "Screw those bastards," but I couldn't shake it. I felt like I made this happen.

For me, it taught a brutal reality: the world isn't fair. Even when you do everything right—by the book—your teeth can still get smashed in. Legitimacy doesn't stand a chance against a badge and a grudge.

Legality—legitimacy—whatever label you slap on it means nothing when the people in power decide not to recognize it. A state-issued permit doesn't stop a political agenda. The law said we were legal. The sheriff — and his allies in the press—said we were criminals. And somewhere between those two truths stood a SWAT team with Kevlar, AR-15s, and a narrative to sell.

The green rush stopped being a business venture. It became a fight for survival.

I didn't know what my next move was, so I called my mentor—my business partner, a lawyer—and asked the simplest question I could: "Who do I call?"

He pointed me toward a high-profile attorney who lived in the same posh neighborhood as him on the Detroit River.

I called while the news replayed our raid on a loop. Over and over. Our arrest was treated like bigger news than the marijuana law passing in the first place. People love blood and guts more than they love compassion and relief.

The fancy lawyer listened, then steered me somewhere else. He said I needed an Oakland County criminal defense attorney—someone built for that courthouse, someone who could handle the spotlight that was already burning a hole through my front door.

When I hung up, I called Neil Rockind. And that same night, I met him at his house—just minutes from mine.

* * *

Nine of us were indicted for selling marijuana—even though the state had made it legal. Two members of the team, equally involved, walked away untouched. Why? Because optics matter. Charging a police officer's soon-to-be wife or a former MLB star's daughter wouldn't serve the narrative. The No Pot Shops campaign needed a clear villain—someone they could crucify in court to scare off other potential dispensary owners.

That villain was us.

Not that I wasn't part of the team—I was. But I was never on surveillance. Never behind the counter. Never made a sale. I was never even present when undercover officers walked into our shop using real drivers licenses and real state-issued medical marijuana cards under fake names to make their purchases. That was the evidence they used to build their case. Legal cards. Real patients on paper. Fictitious names rubber-stamped by the state itself.

It didn't matter.

That was enough for a very willing judge to sign off on arrest warrants. Enough to paint us as criminals instead of caregivers. And just like that, I was charged as a conspirator.

Everyone except Doty's girl—who was never charged—and Mickey's daughter, whose charges were dropped almost immediately.

Tony, Nick's brother, got it worse. Following advice from Ferndale police officers, he legally kept a firearm at the shop for protection. That responsible act landed him a federal gun enhancement. A decade tacked on to his charges — just like that. All for trying to protect his staff, his patients, his family.

The press kept cranking out coverage. FIRST POT SHOP RAIDED IN STATE screamed the headlines.

At a live press conference, Sheriff Bouchard and the county prosecutor stood smugly behind a table stacked with bags of our weed and two of my grandfather's old hunting rifles — claiming we were connected to Mexican drug cartels. He told reporters "This is Michigan — not a Cheech and Chong movie, and it's getting increasingly dangerous."

It was all theater. Misinformation packaged for prime time. But it worked. The media lapped it up. The sheriff got his headlines. The system got its scapegoats. And the public? They started to second guess the law they had just passed—exactly the reaction they wanted.

Meanwhile, I went back to work.

That same morning, still reeling from the raid, I had my assistant send a lease proposal on behalf of a client—the Michigan Supreme Court—for new offices at Ford Field. Ironic, in the oddest sense. A few years later, I would find myself as a defendant before that very same Supreme Court—facing discipline for the case that had just erupted.

Even more awkward, later that same day—while I was picking through the pieces of my house after the cops tore it apart, calling for my cats that had bolted into the neighborhood—a campaign staffer for my best friend showed up.

He was running for a State Senate seat and directed him to pull the campaign sign from my front lawn. It had been caught in the forefront of the news coverage—looped on virtually every local news station in Detroit.

I was on his election committee. I was his best friend. But I understood immediately.

I was toxic.

And I knew in that moment that I was never going to be looked at the same way again.

Days after the raid, an op-ed appeared in the Oakland Press under the headline "Clinical Relief's Open Letter to the Public."

Many have read or heard my name, Ryan Richmond, in the past few days relating to Oakland County Sheriff Bouchard's raid on Clinical Relief's medical marijuana clinic in Ferndale. A friend told me that social change can be accepted by the people much quicker than police actions will let old stereotypes die. If Sheriff Bouchard's parody of Cheech and Chong were true for Clinical Relief then Police Academy 2 on steroids would be true for the Sheriff's department--guns drawn with 8 year olds in the sights, a dragnet that placed truly innocent people in solitary confinement, home searches that were about intimidation as opposed to thoroughness. Fortunately, neither parody is true.

Clinical Relief operates within the law and wants to set the standard for our industry. Sheriff Bouchard simply doesn't like the law because it's too broad. His approach is guilt by association

instead of innocence because of medical benefits. He doesn't respect what two-thirds of Michigan voters decided.

I welcome clarification of Michigan law. Our clinics want to be members of their communities. We have had a criminology class from Eastern Michigan University, Ferndale police and many different municipal leaders pay us a visit, the same offer was extended to Mike. If Sheriff Bouchard has his way: we, you, have no rights even within the law.

I am an entrepreneur and believe that medical marijuana is the next best thing since sliced bread. Let's talk about 7,500 caregivers earning from $10,000 to $60,000 supplying Michigan's medical marijuana needs. That could be 7,500 Michigan families off the unemployment ranks. And, 20,000 less incarcerations, that's probably bad for the policing business.

Protestors outside courthouse as we prepare for trial.

7

Full Steam Ahead

Branded a criminal and stripped of the professional respect I'd spent years building in the business world, I was angry—but I didn't retreat. I doubled down. If they were going to label me a weed dealer, a cartel kingpin, I was going to become the best damn weed dealer in the state.

After the raid, the media fell into lockstep, recycling the No Pot Shops talking points as if they were trying to provoke a war—or maybe just harvest clicks. Either way, the result was the same. Only one outlet came close to getting it right. Just after we got busted, a piece ran based on an interview I'd given weeks earlier to Matt Labash at The Weekly Standard, a national conservative publication. At the end of the article, Matt wrote:

When I call Clinical Relief lawyer Paul Tylenda, he's happy to tell me the usual drug-enforcement horror stories: how the charges are "bulls—," how his clients' homes were ransacked, how their children had guns drawn on them, how the cops even took money out of the kids' piggy banks, how undercover officers posed as patients with proper identification, and how his clients, after making bail, even had to buy back their seized cars from "the Sarge's used car lot." If convicted, his clients could face years in jail for doing what they thought the law permitted, or at least didn't prohibit.

Sheriff Bouchard, when reached by phone, denies the horror stories. He says he's not confused about the law: "There is no place to

35

legally buy marijuana in the state. If there's no place to legally buy medical marijuana, it's illegal to buy medical marijuana." The city of Ferndale smiling on such activities with ordinances doesn't matter to him. "You cannot zone illegal activity into legality, you can no more zone for a dispensary than you can for a cocaine or heroin shop. . . . We're the referees, we enforce the rules. If you don't like the rules, go to Lansing or to the voters and get them changed."

I was never going to make the same mistake twice—trusting the media to tell the whole truth. So I moved carefully, quietly. I dodged reporters and microphones and did what I could in silence: rebuild.

I often forwarded media opportunities to Neil whenever they came my way:

"Neil, the League of Women Voters asked me to speak on May 5th. Despite what you think, I'm trying not to get my name out there or get published. I have no interest in speaking. But this is exactly the kind of group that needs to be educated. Are you interested?"

"I'd be happy to," Neil wrote back.

* * *

We kept our Lansing location open and relaunched in Detroit—across 8 Mile. I was against it from the start. I didn't get into this industry to put anyone in danger. I wanted to help people—patients like my late mom—not operate in a war zone. At that time, that was exactly what Detroit was.

The memory of my Mother and her dealer always stuck with me. She didn't want to get high. She just wanted relief. Safe, consistent, quality relief. And that's what I wanted to build—for people like her.

But Detroit, south of 8 Mile Road didn't feel safe or consistent. It was chaos waiting to happen. My Colorado partners insisted it was the future. I disagreed.

Before I ever moved into cannabis, I'd already been living in Detroit real estate—flipping houses, renovating them, renting them out.

I knew how to move. I knew what had to be done and who had to be paid so your copper pipes didn't disappear overnight. I learned fast that bored teenagers in a neighborhood could be a bigger threat than the homeless guys you see pushing carts.

And everyone I knew grew up on the same parental Detroit warnings, like they were part of the city code: fill your tank before you go downtown. Don't give yourself a reason to stop on the mile roads.

Unless you were trying to score harder drugs, there was no reason to.

Detroit wasn't the only problem. Money was disappearing. Jake and I weren't getting paid—and were being asked to kick in more. So on a Saturday afternoon, the two of us met up at a bar in Clarkston, and over a couple of beers we laid it all out, and made the decision: we'd break off and do it ourselves. We had the knowledge. We had the drive. And when you run a retail dispensary, growers come to you. Product wouldn't be an issue for two guys who couldn't even manage a houseplant.

Our former partners weren't happy, but we didn't see another way forward.

They were busy building their new location—deeper into the chaos—south of Seven Mile. I wished them luck. And because they'd stopped paying their share of the rent and payroll on the struggling Lansing shop, we told them they were off the hook. It wouldn't be their responsibility anymore.

Money talks. So they walked.

Jake and I signed the partnership paperwork together, then headed straight to the bank to open our new business account. Jake would run the day-to-day operations–sweat equity– and I put up a lot of the funds. I still asked him to put a little more skin in the game.

We rebranded our Lansing shop from Clinical Relief of Lansing to the equally boring, yet still medically aligned Relief Choices of Lansing.

Then we found a new location in the suburbs—Warren, MI—close to the old store in Ferndale. The store itself wasn't perfect. It was wedged into a strip mall next to a liquor store and a chicken-and-fish joint that advertised: "You buy, we fry." (More than a catchy slogan: under Michigan law, food stamp (EBT) benefits couldn't be used on hot, prepared meals. But if a customer brought raw food — fish, chicken, shrimp — the store would cook it for them, for free. It was survival capitalism.)

But maybe the wildest part of the location? It sat kitty-corner from the trailer park where Eminem grew up—8 Mile, the movie, the myth, the asphalt scripture. Ground zero. And every time—well, maybe just once—I looked at that corner, I heard his warning, buzzing like a streetlight: "You only get one shot, do not miss your chance to blow."

The spot wasn't ideal in my head, but back then "ideal" didn't mean trendy or pretty. It meant survivable. The alternative meant crossing into Detroit, and every instinct I'd learned flipping houses told me the same thing: don't add extra risk if you don't have to.

Still, the biggest selling point of the location had nothing to do with fried fish or famous rappers.

It was the address—just north of Eight Mile. Not Detroit. And barely twenty feet across the county line from Sheriff Bouchard's turf—the same Oakland County machine that had raided us in Ferndale, dragged our names through the mud, and made me Public Enemy #1.

Back then, while everyone else crowded in south of 8 Mile, that address kept us and our customers safer than any other dispensary in Metro Detroit.

Over time, the Warren dispensary became a safe haven for Metro Detroit patients—people like mom.

But that didn't mean the cops left us alone.

Almost immediately, Warren PD put a target on us. The hostility wasn't subtle. We got raided within the first few weeks—no warrant, no media, no headline. Just a show of force. A message delivered in boots and hand guns: you're not welcome here.

We opened back up anyway.

The mayor made sure the message stayed public. He went to the press and made it clear he didn't like the voter-approved law, repeating the same old script—that people like Jake and me were just organized crime in nicer clothes, that dispensaries were magnets for "undesirables."

Even though he'd been an early mouthpiece in the No Pot Shops army—out there telling voters not to pass the law—the only person who didn't openly oppose us once we launched was Macomb County Prosecutor Eric Smith. And in an irony too perfect to make up, he'd later end up on the wrong side of the law himself.

Ironically, it would later come out that Smith had been embezzling money. Not just any money — but funds taken from drug asset forfeiture accounts. The same pool of cash he urged his officers to raid and replenish. Businesses like ours were the ATM. And Smith? He was the one pocketing the withdrawals.

Seven years after we opened, he'd be convicted and sent to federal prison. But back then, he was the law. And he used every tool he had to keep us afraid and paying.

He sent the county narcotics team to harass our staff and patients. Directed unmarked cars to park in our lot like vultures. Had officers grab cash from our registers and left everything else untouched. Pulled patients over as they left—just to scare them straight. Locked our staff up for a day or two and then—nothing. No charges. No case. Just punishment without paperwork.

All of it while he quietly lined his own pockets with the money we were being robbed of.

Eric Smith stands behind the Macomb County Sheriff as they urge voters to vote no on proposal 1.

In this business, you make strange friends. One of mine was a Warren resident from a prominent Michigan family. He was fascinated by what we were building, and as an entrepreneur he respected the risk—respected that we were doing it out in the open.

After he became a patient and made a purchase, he told the staff who he was and asked to speak with me. He'd read my name in the papers. We hit it off right away.

He also happened to be a very good friend with the Warren police chief and knew of the threats we faced surviving to stay open. His advice and something he arranged?

"Start making monthly donations to the local cops. It'll buy you some breathing room."

So we did.

Cash payments—straight to the Warren Fraternal Order of Police. Hand-delivered by either Jake or I. Escorted by an actual police cruiser, destination unknown—like they were making a bank-deposit run, not handing it over to the spouses of fallen brothers. No receipts. No ledger. No questions asked. That didn't stop us from asking for a receipt—more out of curiosity than expectation. Everyone knew what this was. Even Al Capone would have known what this was.

It didn't stop the raids and threats—at least not completely. But it slowed them down enough to keep our doors open with only minimal disruption.

When the prosecutor, the top cop, leads with greed and intimidation, the whole department learns to speak the same language. The badge becomes a bargaining chip. Justice gets priced out. And what started as a cannabis business—legal, licensed, above board — became something darker.

Bribes. Fees. Permits. Taxes. Favors. Donations. Call them what you want—licensing, compliance, inspections, campaign contributions. It's all part of the same game. Pay to play. And those who don't? They get shut down, zoned out, or regulated to death. This is how I started to learn how business really worked. It became normal—routine—even, and it was the only way we could keep going.

Legality has very little to do with justice. And in this game, the rules are written by the people already cashing in. That's how old money keeps making new money. Don't change a god damn thing.

Our new friend also filled us in on the mayor—who looked more like Mr. Burns from The Simpsons than a seasoned politician. "If you ever need a wild card," he said, "just remind the mayor about the video." The footage, shot by a disgruntled city worker, if it ever came to that, apparently showed the now 60-something-year-old confirmed bachelor kissing another man in a parking lot—an image that could have torched his long-standing political career and reputation in blue-collar, working-class Warren.

We never had to use it.

Just hinting at it was enough. When I called him one day to ask if he would direct his officers to leave us alone, he said:

"Ryan, the residents of Warren do not want a dispensary in their town."

I replied, "I think the residents are more progressive than you give them credit for. At least we're out of the closet and proud of what we sell."

He got the message—and to his credit, I never had a personal problem with him again.

We never had to pay him off. Most of our profits would end up lining the pockets of the county prosecutor and local and county police departments. But we stayed open in Warren—for a while.

Wanting to hold our ground—and grow with the budding industry—Jake and I opened new businesses in other Detroit suburbs like Lincoln Park, Redford, Rochester Hills and Troy.

Part of it was expansion. Part of it was strategy. We figured that if one name lived in a bunch of places, we'd be harder to erase than a single storefront with a single target on its door. And we kept telling ourselves the same thing: someday—hopefully sooner than later—the ridiculous attacks would end.

Some of those locations lasted weeks, others months. Some never made it to opening day—shut down by another sheriff, another crusading prosecutor, another overzealous city council or building inspector. From August 2010 to the end of 2014, we averaged a raid every 26 days.

Every 26 days, armed agents stormed one of our locations or homes.

It crushed our margins. It scared the shit out of our employees. But we kept going.

* * *

Police intimidation didn't scare all of our employees. While other dispensaries obsessed over lab results and terpene charts, we had something that couldn't be quantified—something no spreadsheet could capture.

We had Amanda, Cassie, and Trinity.

They didn't just work the counter. They were the counter. They didn't just turn heads—they held the damn line, and with a mostly male customer base, that mattered more than any marketing plan. Under Jake's leadership they helped steer the ship, and they earned a nickname that started as a joke and turned into a fact: Ryan's Angels. Sharp, stunning, fearless. Stronger than the guys—emotionally, physically, professionally. When some of the men folded at the first whiff of trouble, these women stood ten feet tall.

Because back then, the pool of "dispensary men" was thin and predictable: neck tattoos, long-haired underground hippies, guys who'd been moving ounces since high school, or dudes fresh from their parents' basements smelling like Afghani Kush and unemployment. That was the norm.

And when the raids came—Amanda, Cassie, and Trinity didn't flinch. They stared down rifles and masks. Got cuffed. Hauled in.

Booked. Jailed. Then showed up the next day like it was business as usual.

* * *

By then, my commercial real estate business had collapsed to nothing.

The phone stopped ringing. Clients I'd worked with for years disappeared overnight. No callbacks. No deals. No new leads. The ongoing prosecution tied to the Ferndale dispensary arrest had scorched whatever reputation I had left in the industry. Who wants to do business with a guy looking at the possibility of a 20-year felony sentence?

No one wanted their name tied to mine anymore. I went from respected businessman to radioactive overnight—the kind of fallout that lingers long after the headlines fade. Even the man I called my mentor—kept his distance. And I didn't blame him.

He didn't say it outright, but I knew respect—and legitimacy—mattered to him. Mattered to everyone, I thought. So I did the right thing.

I didn't wait for the conversation. I just walked away.

Walking away from him, and other peers I respected was the only part that hurt. Not the job, not the clients, not the industry—I'd already let go of all that. But losing their guidance and friendship? That stung. Still, I knew I was toxic. No one needed to be in my world. And I wasn't about to drag anyone else I cared about down with me.

And yet, getting forced out of that role—out of that company, out of that industry—was the reset I didn't know I needed. I hated being a broker. I was good at it, sure. But the grind, the fakeness, the constant chase for commissions—it wore me down.

Even my wife noticed. One night, in the middle of everything falling apart, she said, "You know, you were miserable as a broker. Life sucks right now, but… you actually seem happier."

And she was right. I was broke, under indictment, and facing years in prison.

But for the first time in a long time, I wasn't pretending. The truth is, maybe I even enjoyed it—the excitement, the grenades being hurled at me—like only a shell-shocked veteran learns to crave.

Still, I kept telling my wife, "Once we get through this—once the cops accept this new law and the state finally gets its act together—we'll be in a better position."

I believed it. I had to.

A patient entering the front door of our Relief Choices dispensary in Warren.

The front lobby of Relief Choices in Warren, where patients filled paperwork, verified their status, and waited to purchase medical cannabis.

Jake weighs out a bag of medical cannabis for a patient from the counter.

CANNALOCK
SMELL PROOF BAG TECHNOLOGY

100% SMELL PROOF BAGS. WE BELIEVE EVERY ONE SHOULD ENJOY THEIR PRIVACY.

SMELL PROOF EFFECTIVENESS

Cannalock Bags	99.5%
Turkey Bags	91%
Smell Proof Plastic Bags	82%
Zip Lock Bags	48%

CHARCOAL

We use an oxygen activated charcoal liner in all of our products, providing no smell detection.

GUARANTEE

We guarantee our results, our bags (not duffel bags) come with a 100% money back guarantee against any defects.

LEADERS

Our innovative design and production feature can ensure results longer and stronger than any one else in the market.

MADE IN USA

We manufacture, assemble, promote and ship all of our products proudly within the United States. Global reach, local impact.

Cannalock Duffel Bag $759.99

Cannalock Large Bag $59.99

Cannalock Medium Bag $49.99

Cannalock Small Bag $39.99

CANNALOCK.COM

A bag we sold at the dispensary, designed to help contain the smell, made from the same material used in my military-issued chemical warfare suit.

relief *choices*

Our Kind Baked marijuana infused edibles line.

8

The Love of My Life

By 2006, I had a career as a stockbroker and a mortgage company I ran with my friend. My team handled conforming loans—good-credit, by-the-book deals. Kevin's half of the office specialized in the economically advantaged.

That's when I met Sarah. She is as pretty as the sun reflecting on the lake.

She is smaller than me and even smaller once the high heels come off—the same heels that carried her into the bar the night we first met. She is delicate. Her brown hair is darker than the girls I'd dated before. Smart in a way that showed up on paper and in conversation—straight A's in high school and college—and she is the nicest person you could imagine without it feeling like an act.

Her mom and dad raised her and her brother in a middle-class neighborhood where people knew where they came from. They knew their family's history. They worked hard. Her mom, a now retired school teacher. Her dad was third-generation owner of a successful clothing store with locations across Michigan. Then malls and Walmart moved in and it collapsed. He filed bankruptcy and went back for his master's degree, thinking the corporate world would be ready for a 45-year-old newly-minted marketing graduate.

When we met Sarah was working at an advertising agency, chasing the career her dad never got the chance to have. She stayed late.

She got paid less than the men her age and did what it took anyway. I was proud of her. Her bosses were too.

When the agency folded in Detroit, nearly 500 people were let go. Five stayed. And one of them was a 26-year-old account executive—smart, relentless, and impossible to ignore.

I was always afraid of getting married. I never thought I would. I didn't want to get backed into a corner like my parents—two people who stayed too long in something that should've never happened in the first place. I didn't want to be the reason, again, for a marriage that should never have been.

But when I met Sarah, I knew right away this was different. Something I never would've—could've—imagined.

She had a good heart. And she never judged me for who I was. She didn't flinch at my rough edges. She didn't ask me to pretend. She supported me whether it was real estate or cannabis. She just stood there, steady, like she'd been made just for me, and I for her.

We got married on a beach in Saint Lucia. I wore a white dress shirt and linen pants. When she walked down that aisle of palm leaves, she took my breath away.

None of my family showed up. Sarah's did. They always were present—this constant thread running through her life, and then, somehow, stitched into the second half of mine.

We moved into a three-bedroom brick house that made Sarah cry the first time she walked through it. She stood in the entryway like she had entered Fred Sanford's home. I told her, "Trust me. We can make money here."

We were the second owners of a 1947 Sears catalog home. We renovated and replaced almost everything—room by room, paycheck by paycheck—until it stopped being a house and became ours. And then, eventually, it became too small for the family we were already making space for in our heads.

And I was right.

We did make good money on that house.

When it came time for kids—when we finally put our professional lives in the back seat—the worst thing happened.

Before her 29h birthday, Sarah was already coming apart. Slowing down. Constant pain. And—just like my mom—she hid it from the world so well that I was the only one who really saw what it cost her.

Doctors called it "arthritis," which, from where I was standing, always sounded like a made-up catch-all. A polite label for something hurts—no mystery solved, no real plan, just a word that let everyone move on.

Sarah didn't move on. She tried everything. Acupuncture. Australian-style chiropractic therapy. A daily diet of ibuprofen just to get through work. By dinner, she was wiped out—spent like someone who'd run a marathon nobody else could see.

I even convinced her to try an infused cookie one day when things got really bad. Sarah had never been a weed person—not from what I'd ever seen. It wasn't her thing. She was skeptical, but by then she was willing to try anything.

The cookies came from the dispensary: two small chocolate chip cookies sealed together in one package.

She ate one.

Then she ate the other.

A little while later, she locked herself in the bedroom.

"You ate them both?" I asked through the door.

In my opinion, they worked—she was so high and so paranoid she barely had time to think about her pain. Sarah disagreed. She called in "stoned" the next day just to make sure the paranoia was fully gone.

And then I crossed paths with a man some of the world's smartest doctors considered the world's most renowned rare-pain doctor. He'd roll into our parking lot in a Model S Tesla and made big, frequent purchases—big enough that, from the outside, you'd think he was reselling.

He wasn't.

He was giving it away to patients—the ones he truly cared about, the ones whose suffering didn't respond to degrees, accolades, or whatever was framed on his wall.

I asked the staff, "Who is this guy making these huge purchases?"

"He's a doctor," they said.

The internet told me he was more than that. He was one of the country's top rare pain docs.

So I did what I do best: I skipped the chain of command. I waited for his usual pickup time and ambushed him in the room where we sold weed out of converted glass jewelry cases—with mason jars lined up like candy, and a cash register on the counter.

Maybe he was more impressed by me—the risks I'd taken to help people, people like his patients—than I was with him. Because when I told him about Sarah, about the dead ends and the exhaustion, about how pain had shrunk her life, he didn't give me the usual speech. He didn't tell me to have her "call the office."

He said he'd see her.

Tomorrow.

Or any day she wanted.

Sarah was in disbelief. She was used to specialists booking months out—doctors with half Mitch's credentials and none of his reputation acting like they were doing you a favor by returning a call.

She got in right away. Two visits, a referral, more imaging—real investigation, not guesswork. What everyone had chalked up to a back injury turned out to be arthritic hips ground down to the sockets. Both of them. Something no one had found in three years.

She would need both hips replaced.

And because you can't replace both at the same time, it meant a long recovery between surgeries—more than a year of rehab, pain management, re-learning how to move through the world. And then do it all over with the left side.

It pushed everything back.

Including the family we wanted. Further into the future.

9

Planting Change, Not Protests

When Michigan passed its medical marijuana law and was instantly opposed by the resistance, I didn't grab a protest sign or a bullhorn. I didn't march on the Capitol steps or chant outside courthouses. That wasn't my style. I wasn't in this to shout—I was in this to build.

My form of advocacy wasn't loud, but it was relentless. It lived in commercial leases, municipal approvals, messaging, and staff training. It lived in staying open—reopening after every raid, reinvesting after every seizure, and never once backing down. While some activists and former dispensary owners, victimized by the system, stood on the Capitol lawn or in front of court houses with signs and bull horns, I was in backrooms negotiating with landlords, city planners, and legal teams. Jake and I turned defiance into infrastructure. We built where they tried to destroy.

And in doing so, we became more dangerous to the "No Pot Shops" crowd than any protest line ever could.

Truth is, I never fit in with the protest crowd.

I didn't come from the world of cannabis reform—the tie-dye, jam bands, drum circles. I wasn't smoking at the Diag during Hash Bash or livestreaming city council meetings. I wore suits. Jake ran spreadsheets. We tracked inventory. He calculated margins. We were business—all business.

I wanted the same outcomes as the movement. I just didn't always buy the tactics—or the tone. I wasn't chasing rebellion. I was chasing legitimacy.

Early in the green rush, somebody called a meeting after Attorney General Schuette leaned on his old friends in the Court of Appeals and bad case law started rolling downhill. It was one of those key players only sit-downs—half summit, half mafia movie.

The goal was simple: the antagonists were talking, the papers were printing, and law enforcement was loving the spotlight. We needed one voice. One message. One plan.

A room full of entrepreneurs is hard enough to organize—it's like herding cats. A room full of early cannabis entrepreneurs? That was herding fireworks.

But we sat down anyway. The meeting was "called to order," and less than two minutes later joints were flying around the room in every direction.

I didn't want to be the only guy saying no—the stiff in the suit, the buzzkill. So I passed one to the left. And immediately another appeared from the right. Longer. Fatter. Like the room had decided my job wasn't strategy—it was to keep the rotation alive.

That was a lot of the meeting. Puff. Puff. Give.

No agenda. No structure. No assignments. No plan. No strategy. No coordination. Just a graceful little dance of zigzags and kush while our "unified message" disappeared into the ceiling.

Looking back, the real question isn't why we lost ground. It's why we thought we were fighting at all.

None of us knew politics. None of us knew lobbying. None of us knew PR, crisis messaging, or how to build a coalition that could survive a coordinated attack. Any effort would've been clumsy—probably embarrassing, maybe even useless. But it could've moved us all forward a little quicker.

So I stuck to what I know. Keep growing. Keep selling. Every bag of weed sold, every new store was another branch pushing deeper into the state's legal, economic, and cultural landscape. Each one was a silent but unignorable argument for legitimacy.

But I didn't stop at storefronts.

Behind the scenes, I worked on policy. Legitimacy. Each year we were in business, Jake pulled together sales data and patient demographics, and I wrote a white paper on the economic, regulatory, and public-health impacts of medical marijuana in Michigan. It was distributed to members of the state legislature—clear, data-driven, and solution-oriented. Not a manifesto, but a roadmap. And at a time when there was zero transparency in the industry.

It wasn't presented on my behalf, but under an alias—a fiction: the Michigan Dispensary Association. What the power structure didn't realize was that "association" was basically Jake, me, and my cats.

I organized what I could, wild-ass-guessed the rest, and published my best shot at the truth. I even built a website—dispensaryassociation.org—and at night, with my cats walking across the keyboard, I worked behind the curtain like the Wizard. During the day I was the public face—Dorothy—smiling, explaining, pretending I wasn't terrified of what might be waiting on the other side of the curtain.

With that document in hand, I walked the halls of the Capitol alongside a professional lobbyist from one of Lansing's most respected firms.

Scott—one of the coolest guys I'd ever met—moved through the building like he owned the place. We met with key legislators and leadership, sat across from decision-makers, and I explained how the industry could function—safely, effectively—if they'd only let it grow.

"They really like you around here," I said. "With term limits, I've been in Lansing longer than a lot of these guys combined."

But I could feel the angle. A lot of those backdoor meetings weren't designed to make progress—maybe just to satisfy curiosity, to ask the questions politicians didn't want on the record. And for Scott, I was probably bait: a foot in the door, a compelling story he could trade up into a better client, a real paying client and their demands for the state government.

Still, the meetings did something for me. They fed the same craving I'd been dragging around for years—legitimacy. Me, in the Capitol, shaking hands, speaking policy, treated like I belonged.

Those conversations may not have flipped anyone overnight. But they did shift the tone. And I still believe—at least in some small way—they helped the industry. They gave it something we both required: legitimacy.

Some people fought from the outside. I walked straight through the front door of power in Lansing. In the end, we were all doing what we thought was best—fighting the good fight the only way we knew how.

10

The Mouthpiece

After my first arrest, my lawyer Neil and even our former County CEO, Mr. Patterson, both told me the same thing: "You've got a PR problem. That's your biggest challenge." They weren't wrong. Prosecutors and police weren't just raiding dispensaries.

They were raiding the narrative—holding press conferences, flooding the papers with soundbites, rewriting the story before we even had a chance to speak. If we didn't build our own megaphone, the public would never hear our side.

So Jake and I tried—again—to build legitimacy. Not with permission slips or lobbyists, but with our own words, and the coding skills I'd picked up back in my real-estate days.

We bought the domain: marijuanapatients.org.

At first it was modest. Just a simple site.

But the site did something the mainstream wouldn't: it told the truth as we saw it. It carried the stories the medical marijuana community actually wanted—without the cheap bias, without the "reefer madness" tone, without treating patients like punchlines. It gave people information they needed if they were considering cannabis as an alternative to the mainstream—real guidance, real context, not scare tactics.

And then it grew. Fast.

Thousands of visitors a day. Hundreds of thousands of followers on social. This was before legalization started sweeping the map—back when fewer than twelve states even had medical marijuana laws, and everybody else—from New York to Kentucky to Idaho—was still trapped under prohibition.

People were starved for real information. And MPO became an outlet. A lifeline. A place where they didn't have to be talked down to just to learn the basics.

Back then, the alternatives were thin. High Times was mostly stoner gossip mixed with legalization advocacy—best water bong, thirty ways to get stoned, political hit pieces, that kind of thing. Cheech and Chong were comedy. What didn't exist was a clearinghouse for medical research, legislative updates, and stories from patients and their weed dealers fighting to survive inside a broken system. MPO filled that vacuum, and people poured in. It offered legitimacy we were after.

Jake, our lawyer friend Paul and I were the official board members, but truthfully, the site was my unpaid job after work let out. I wrote most of the copy, solicited articles, and answered emails at midnight. We had a revolving door of contributors—doctors and lawyers eager for bylines. Some cared about patients. Most cared more about their careers. I didn't care why they wrote. I cared that patients finally had information.

But MPO wasn't just a bulletin board—it became a weapon. And weapons get noticed.

We published pieces that called out hypocrisy. Like Sheriff Bouchard—always ready to grandstand about "protecting families," while his office fattened its budget with forfeiture money seized from cancer patients. We turned the lens back on the politicians who acted untouchable.

It pissed them off—which told me it was working. And it told me something else, too: they were reading.

At one point we got a cease-and-desist letter from the Oakland County legal department—one of the same agencies prosecuting me. Our offense? We'd cropped a marijuana leaf into the county's copyright protected oak tree logo to go with an article exposing their bizarre drug-testing tactics. The labs they leaned on were notorious for junk science, and we called it what it was—before investigators caught on and the wider media finally exposed the scheme.

They didn't want a correction. They wanted silence.

We framed the letter and kept publishing. But we took the image down. Not because they were right—because it wasn't a fight worth picking, not with a war still ahead of us.

Ironically, our biggest hit wasn't some polished academic piece. It was a video and article called "How to Smoke a Water Bong" that gained millions of eyeballs. A stoner tutorial disguised as a Trojan horse. People were drawn in by the clickbait, but once inside, they were exposed to stories about raids, medical info, laws, and hypocrisy.

And that terrified the status quo. Because prohibition only survives in the dark. It feeds on ignorance, on silence. Education and exposure are its worst enemies. MPO was pulling back the curtain, and I saw it working.

Our articles—and the website—started showing up in the papers. It popped in Google searches too, sometimes above the damning hit pieces we were trying to correct. For a while it felt like the search engines were using us as the footnote of record—like when the noise got loud enough, even the internet came looking for the cleanest version of the truth.

We also became a magnet for professionals who could read the room. The smarter ones saw the writing on the wall—and they wanted to be positioned when the wave hit.

Lawyers especially. They wanted their names out there, their phones ringing, ready to cash in on new clients—because law enforcement was still tripling down on raids and asset forfeiture across the state. Both sides saw real money in medical cannabis.

Just not for the same reasons.

Doctors wrote articles, hoping to attract patients for certifications—the legal loophole that let us sell weed through prescriptions.

Everyone had a motive, but the site didn't discriminate. If the work pushed forward education or legitimacy, we ran it. Eventually, we let doctors advertise and pay for placement. The money wasn't some payday—it kept the lights on. It paid for hosting, maintenance, and the costs to attend industry trade shows and keep building the network.

The site also became a testing ground for ideas I would later turn into products. "No Smell," a bag made from the same material used in the chemical warfare suit I was once issued, and used to mask the smell of cannabis, started as a blog ad. So did Hemp Well—back then, an obscure product built around CBD, an acronym most people didn't recognize. MPO gave me a platform to test, to experiment, to turn ideas into realities.

Looking back, MPO was more than a website. It was the first real proof that I could control my own story—or at least grab the wheel and change the trajectory a little. That I didn't have to let the government define me as a criminal. That I could fight prohibition not just with court cases and surviving raids, but with truth.

And I believe that was another reason they came after me so hard. Because if you want to win a war like

that, you don't just raid storefronts—you attack legitimacy. You attack the people telling the truth.

The Marijuana Patients Organization at a medical cannabis convention. The event was later raided by the Detroit Police Department after organizers planned an area where patients could consume their medicine.

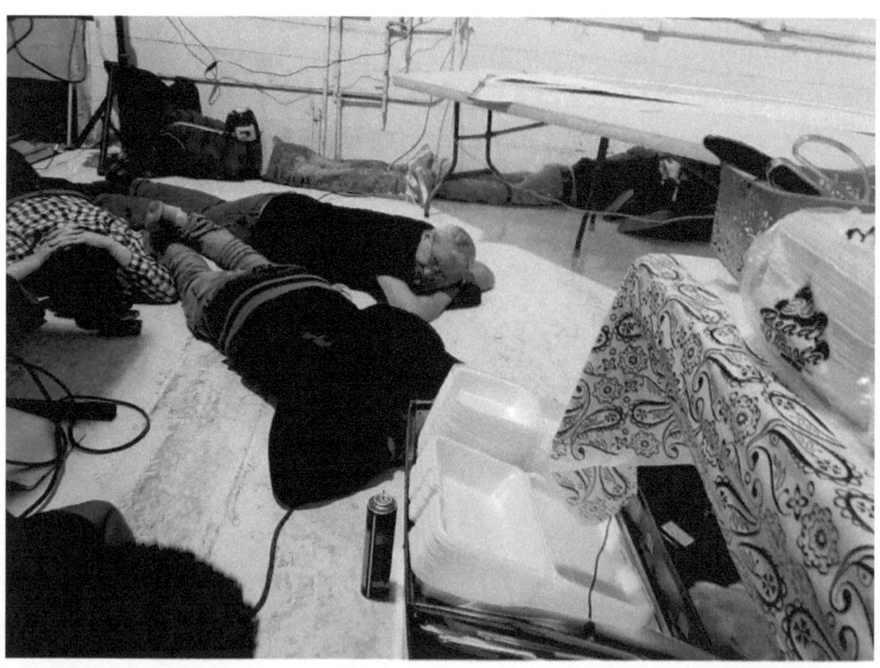

<h1 style="text-align:center">11</h1>

Who Called The Lawyer

Almost two years after we opened the Warren location, I got the call. It was a perfect Michigan summer day—bright, warm—right around lunchtime.

"Ryan, hurry up—we're getting raided."

I bolted from my Royal Oak office, ten minutes away, and hit the road. By then, raids weren't a surprise. If anything, it was weird when they didn't happen. But something felt off this time.

When I pulled up, only one vehicle sat out front: a rusted-out Michigan State Police Suburban. No convoy. No tactical van. Just that one tired truck, idling like bait.

From the parking lot, I called Neil—my lawyer, who had branded himself as the state's foremost marijuana defense expert after representing me in most of my state trials, and a few friends of mine. He always answered my calls. We were great customers for his criminal defense practice.

"Ryan, don't go in that building. Promise me."

I rarely took Neil's advice. If I listened to him I would have already been out of the game and back in real estate.

"If I don't call you in an hour, let my wife know—and have her get the bail money ready."

I threw on my suit coat, flipped my phone to record, and walked inside.

The place was eerily still. A man in tactical gear approached—he looked more like muscle-for-hire than law enforcement.

"Who are you?" he barked.

I didn't answer. Neil's golden rule: never talk to cops. Not even the ones pretending to be helpful.

He asked again, louder, and pulled a ski mask over his face. Then he turned and shouted to the back of the shop, where my staff sat, hands zip-tied together.

"Who called the fuckin' lawyer?!"

He claimed he had everyone's phones—but someone had gotten a call out. "Who called the fucking lawyer?" he yelled again, angrier now, convinced that I was the fuckin' lawyer.

I stayed calm. "Can I see a warrant? What agency are you with?"

Two more masked men joined him. Same questions: Who was I, and why was I there? I repeated my request—warrant, agency name. They ignored me.

"Wrap it up, boys!" someone shouted.

They tossed bags of product and money into the back of the Suburban, jumped in, and peeled out like bank robbers—not law enforcement.

Neil's calls lit up my phone. I finally answered and told him what happened. And then emailed him later that evening.

Thanks for fielding calls today. Talked with Tylenda and another dispensary owner. Sounds like Dutch is a crooked narcotics cop, has hit up a few disp along the strip in recent weeks. No warrants. Paul thinks the MI state police car was just for show.

Will deliver audio/video to your office in the morning. It's on thumb drive and sounds pretty legible from the little I saw with the IT guy. We know the drill from here, hurry up and wait. And will let you hold/review as our lawyer should it impact us. Hoping it just was just crooked cops and appreciate any thoughts... Thanks again.

Later we learned who they really were—members of a dirty, now-disbanded Detroit narcotics unit with federal intel ties. Think Training Day the movie, only uglier. They'd already hit multiple shops south of 8 Mile, plus two other raids we'd managed to survive. But we were north—outside their turf. This wasn't policing; it was a stickup. A show of force ordered by the federal shadow network working behind the scenes to kneecap the industry.

But the crew pushed it further than their handlers ever asked. We were just one stop on their criminal tour. And by then, I'd started to treat it like weather—just another day. Some days it rained. Some days it didn't.

* * *

Years later I would read in the newspaper about those masked men, that Detroit Police Lieutenant David Hansberry and Officer Bryan Watson were eventually unmasked. In July 2016, a federal jury found them guilty of conspiring to extort and rob drug dealers—using their badges and police tactics to orchestrate fake traffic stops, steal money, drugs, and personal property.

In February 2017, Federal Judge Linda Parker sentenced Hansberry to 12½ years and Watson to 9 years in federal prison. Another member of the crew, Officer Napier, never made it to trial. Under FBI investigation, he shot himself in the head in his parents' driveway.

Not to quote a line from a movie, but I remember thinking: I'd like to believe the last thing that went through his mind—besides that bullet—was the fake lawyer who videotaped him in that dispensary lobby.

Their hustle started with a dealer named Gary Jackson, who tipped them off to a $3 million cartel stash house hoping for a cut. After the raid, Jackson got nothing. When he confronted them, they paid him $250,000 from police asset-forfeiture funds to keep quiet—and demanded more tips.

Jackson recorded them saying things like, "If you work for me, you get out of jail free," and "You could be a millionaire doing this." The deal was simple: give up other drug operations, stay out of jail, and make money with dirty cops.

When another dealer got "raided." They found $300,000 in cash, cocaine, and guns—then made no arrests. Later, in a strip club booth, the same dealer offered them $100,000 and five keys (kilograms of cocaine) for immunity. The crew took the deal.

At trial, Hansberry and Watson argued these weren't acts of extortion. The court didn't buy it. This was systemic abuse of power—organized crime in uniform.

Dutch—the only white guy, the ringleader—was never charged, never questioned, never brought to justice. He kept right on terrorizing patients and shaking down drug dealers like the rules were for everyone else.

* * *

Back at the shop, I cut the zip ties off my staff—though not before I made a few questionable jokes about their current predicament. Then they walked me through what happened.

Cassie said, "They waited until a patient left and then just ran in." Nobody saw them in the windows or on the cameras. Our front door had a locking mechanism—we had to buzz people in—so they waited until it was already open.

"They pulled guns and went straight to the back," she said. Fast.

The thugs stormed in and started snatching phones like that was the first rule of their playbook. But Amanda—quick-thinking as ever—managed to get a call and a text out from the processing room. That's how I found out.

The veteran girls—Ryan's Angels—kept their cool like they always did. But our new guy, Matt, cracked. He gave up everything—like the location of our Rochester Hills warehouse, where we kept the grow and the edibles kitchen: pot brownies, gummy bears, the whole menu.

They leaned on him hard. Told him they'd raid his mom's house. Told him they'd drag her off to jail right alongside him if he didn't co-operate. Matt panicked.

Matt—Jake's cousin—never told us what he said during questioning. Not then, not after. We only learned the truth later, when Dan—Jake's brother—pulled the store's security footage and listened to the audio he'd installed.

We were compromised.

Jake called me in a panic and said we needed to meet. Now. We sat in a bar halfway between my house and his, nursing drinks and watching the room—checking shoulders, clocking new faces—in a place neither of us ever went.

Jake and I didn't wait.

That same night—around 1 a.m.—after renting a moving truck, we drove to the warehouse, and tore it down. We destroyed the younger, less valuable, vegetating plants by stuffing them into garbage bags and dumping them in commercial dumpsters that weren't even ours—other businesses in the industrial complex.

And whatever we thought still had value—the older, more mature, skunky plants—we moved to Jake's pole barn.

The grow wasn't illegal, but we weren't about to give dirty cops another payday—or another chance to twist the story. Looking back, maybe we could've left it. No charges ever came from that raid. And they never came back—that time. But we knew better.

When masked men in police gear rob you at gunpoint, you don't stick around for round two. Whatever trust we'd grown up with—the idea the system was fair, that it worked—was pretty much already gone by then.

Before reporting to prison, Bryan Watson and David Hansberry sit for an interview and make their case against the prosecutions that sent them there.

Deadline Detroit

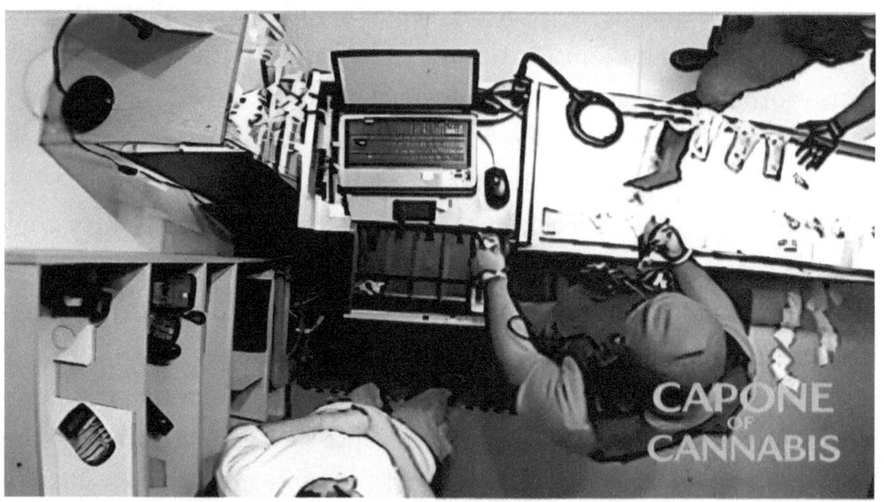

Several of our raid videos can be found at CaponeOfCannabis.com

12

Marijuana Meets Housing Discrimination

Coming from a real estate background—and as someone who's always tried to treat people with basic respect—I was bothered by a few news articles and an op-ed I ran across. They featured Laura Schlecte, a real estate broker and elected official in Jackson, Michigan, openly encouraging landlords to discriminate against tenants who were legally using medical marijuana. She'd put it in writing, and the papers quoted her extensively.

That wasn't ignorance. That was cruelty, wrapped in authority. And it pissed me off.

Her words made me think of my mom—renting her apartment, using cannabis, trying to get through her days like anyone else.

I never made a good landlord. I was "too nice," and I had a soft spot—especially for single moms. I'd let rent slide. I'd wait until the tax refund hit so they could catch up. I'd go out of my way to help the people living in houses I owned.

Part of it was empathy. Part of it was practical—I didn't want anyone desperate enough to wreck the place. But over time you learn a hard truth: the good guys don't always outlast the landlords who don't care.

Laura wasn't just making a business decision. She was smuggling her personal bias into the lease—deciding how her tenants and other tenants should live, what they were allowed to use to cope, what kind of relief they deserved. And if she wanted to play "concerned landlord," you'd think her real worry would've been alcohol, not pot—because if you're talking pure damage, booze is the one that smashes fists through drywall and drags property value down with it.

In a world where cops could kick your door for a plant, where prosecutors could erase your life's work with a signature, Schlecte's words poured gasoline on a fire that was already burning hot. But unlike the others, she wasn't wearing a badge. She didn't have a gun.

Which meant I could push back without looking over my shoulder. Or hiring another lawyer.

So I took my shot.

I filed a formal grievance with the National Association of RE-ALTORS®, citing Mrs. Schlecte's conduct as a clear violation of the NAR Code of Ethics, specifically Article 10, which prohibits discrimination against individuals with disabilities. Unfortunately, the board chose not to pursue disciplinary action, but the message was still delivered—and the public record now reflects it.

Dear Grievance Committee:

I am writing to report the unethical conduct of Laura D. Schlecte. Mrs. Schlecte is the broker/owner of Thinking Real Estate (f/k/a Prudential Premier Properties), located in Jackson. I believe that Mrs. Schlecte has violated Article 10 of the Code of Ethics, and more specifically Standard of Practice 10-3, because she has repeatedly manifested her intent to discriminate against handicapped individuals who are lawful users of medical marijuana under the Michigan Medical Marihuana Act ("MMMA"), MCL §333.26421 et seq., Initiated Law 1 (2008).

Mrs. Schlecte has stated that Jackson residents should be able to use and grow medical marijuana on residential property, as permitted under Michigan law, so long as she does not own or manage the property. In other words, Mrs. Schlecte has stated that property being sold or managed by Thinking Real Estate should be exempt from state law. This inconsistent stance demonstrates that Mrs. Schlecte would prefer to discriminate against handicapped tenants who are using medication necessary to the preservation and maintenance of their health, if state law allowed it (to be clear, it does not).

As a Jackson City Councilwoman, Mrs. Schlecte has acted upon her discriminatory beliefs by supporting a city ordinance that would require a tenant to receive landlord permission before growing medical marijuana in their residence. This provision was ultimately stripped from the ordinance after several attorneys informed her that the provision she supported violates the MMMA. She also publicly stated, "as a landlord I would like to be able to control if my tenants can smoke [marijuana] or not." Mrs. Schlecte ignores the fact that requiring disclosure of medical conditions as a condition precedent to the sale/lease of residential property violates well-settled public policy and both state and federal civil rights laws. Furthermore, Mrs. Schlecte has admitted that not all users of medical marijuana smoke marijuana.

Indeed, many users prefer to ingest marijuana, as smoking, especially smoking, may be detrimental to one's health. However, a landlord cannot prevent a tenant from using lawful medication as prescribed by a doctor, especially when the landlord targets marijuana users alone. Mrs. Schlecte's statements show an acute insensitivity to vulnerable members of our community. No one denies that marijuana is stigmatized. But the scientific and medical community has repeatedly recognized marijuana as a legitimate treatment for several medical conditions including physical and mental disabilities. As a state and a community, we engaged in an important discussion that touched upon the most fundamental justification for the existence of government— protecting the health, safety, and welfare of our citizens. Michigan voters endorsed the scientific and medical communities' view by passing the Michigan Medical

Marihuana Act, which sought to protect a patient's ability to safely access medical marijuana. None of this has deterred Mrs. Schlecte from engaging in immature, unprofessional, and unethical behavior.

In addition to the previous comments, Mrs. Schlecte has asserted that, "Having marijuana in a neighborhood decreases property values". This statement is patently false and unsupported by either facts or data. This statement arguably constitutes the illegal practice of blockbusting – exploiting the fear of declining property values to induce a real estate transaction from which a person may [emphasis added] benefit financially or otherwise. As a REALTOR®, Mrs. Schlecte must be cognizant of the truthfulness of statements she makes regarding property values, especially when such statements become widely circulated by the media in print and electronic form.

Through her actions, Mrs. Schlecte has shown contempt and disregard for state and federal law. She has damaged the goodwill that other REALTORS® in Jackson have built through their involvement with the community. That goodwill has real value. I associate the REALTOR® brand with the things that matter most to me in my everyday life: my family, my friends, and my community—basically, the things closest to my home. Through her words and actions, Mrs. Schlecte is marginalizing and hurting people that I love and care deeply about. These aren't degenerates or drug addicts, but people trying to manage chronic health conditions and cope with daily pain. Some are being treated for cancer. The people I personally know are upstanding members in the Jackson community. My point in saying all of this is to bring some humanity to this letter, and to show that her unprofessional actions and words have real-world consequences.

As a politician, I suppose it makes sense for her to say such things. Elections are about distinguishing yourself from the other candidates. Mrs. Schlecte has taken ownership over this whole marijuana controversy and is crusading on it. But she forgets that while this behavior might be acceptable for a politician campaigning for office, it is not acceptable for a licensed REALTOR®. In all things, REALTORS must exercise their professional conduct, but especially when dealing with contentious issues such as medical marihuana usage in residential real estate. I believe Mrs. Schlecte is entitled to her opinions, but as a REALTOR®, she has voluntarily agreed to abide by the Code of Ethics as a condition of her professional affiliation.

As a REALTOR®, Mrs. Schlecte owes a duty to the public higher than that imposed by state and federal law. Mrs. Schlecte has, in my opinion, repeatedly breached both the letter and spirit of the Code of Ethics promulgated by the National Association of REALTORS®. Her statements concerning the adverse effects upon property value caused by users of medical marihuana demonstrate a reckless disregard for the truth.

This is especially troubling given her myriad REALTOR® accreditations and professional accomplishments. Simply put, she should know better. I believe her behavior has repeatedly fallen below minimum professional and ethical standards. I ask that you look into this, come to your own informed decision as to the appropriateness of Mrs. Schlecte's words and actions as a REALTOR®, and take whatever corrective action you deem appropriate.

Jackson, Michigan, has long been a cautionary tale. At one point it recorded one of the highest drug-induced death rates not only in Michigan but across the entire U.S., ranking 30th nationally. And yet, while opioids hollowed out communities, politicians like her chose to focus their energy on discrimination and attacking cannabis. That kind of misplaced crusade doesn't solve problems — it escalates them.

Schlecte never publicly addressed medical marijuana again, nor did she grant any further interviews on the topic. Whether she learned her lesson is unclear—but I believe the message was received loud and clear.

I'd like to think the voters remembered my letter, because when she ran for mayor a few years later, they said no. But if I'm being honest, it probably had more to do with the oldest rule in politics: "The price good men pay for indifference to public affairs is to be ruled by evil men."

13

High Secrets: The CIA, Weed, and Privacy

The CIA, aligned with corporate interests, has a long history of toppling foreign governments, sidelining politicians, and neutralizing disruptors—often to protect U.S. companies operating abroad.

Their mission—foreign and domestic—is simple: destroy legitimacy. Discredit any person or idea that threatens the interests of the people who already own the game.

So when the same kind of corporate logic showed up at home—aimed at our medical marijuana business because it threatened entrenched interests—it almost felt predictable. And the media, in its own way, ends up serving corporate interests too—whether those interests are overseas or right here at home.

The media coverage back during the early dispensary days leaned on what the Attorney General, Sheriff or Prosecutor thought—their talking points, their bias—because that's where the access was. We weren't always painted as villains, but we weren't exactly treated like legitimate operators either. The stories landed in that gray zone: not a hit piece, not a fair shake—just enough doubt to keep the public uneasy and the system and advertisers comfortable.

Before I stopped talking to reporters—unless it was on my terms, like an op-ed—a longtime Detroit News writer said something to me that finally made it click. "We're all on your side," he told me. "We smoked more pot in college dorm rooms than you could ever sell." Then he lowered his voice and added the real sentence: "But if we cross that d-bag Sheriff, we won't get access to the next murder investigation or the next big story."

And that's how it works—whether the story is about me, or something "bigger," like weapons of mass destruction in Iraq.

Why would the CIA—or any "shadow government"—care about two guys selling medical marijuana in Michigan? We weren't running guns. Unless you asked Sheriff Bouchard we weren't laundering cartel money. We were two guys in a strip mall handing out relief to chemo patients and people with chronic pain. And yet what it felt like—what the raids looked like—wasn't routine policing. It was theater. Pressure. A warning.

The only way it began to make sense—to me—was to stop thinking about drugs as morality and start thinking about them the way power thinks about them: as leverage. Drugs create cash economies, informants, asset forfeiture, courthouse revenue, wiretaps, compromised people, publicly traded prisons, convenient pretexts, and endless "security" narratives. Once you see that, medical cannabis stops being "safe" and starts looking like a system problem—money moving outside approved channels.

And I didn't get there by watching YouTube. I got there the hard way—by living through it, and by reading what the government itself eventually admitted it had done.

MK-ULTRA. Safehouses. Unwitting Americans dosed with LSD in the name of "behavioral research"—a program marketed as science, but driven by a darker obsession: behavior modification. The CIA chased the idea that the mind could be bent, rewritten, steered—through drugs, deprivation, suggestion—until a person said what you wanted, did what you wanted, became what you needed for the story. And if you couldn't control an opponent, there was always the next-best option: contaminate them. Drug them. Disorient them. Ruin their credibility and let the public do the rest.

Operation CHAOS—when the agency quietly built files on Americans: activists, civil-rights leaders (MLK), journalists, student groups—then fed the machine with rumors and manufactured "facts" meant to discredit them, until the Church Committee dragged enough of it into the light that the country couldn't pretend it was all just paranoia anymore.

Propaganda Campaigns that helped destabilize and ultimately topple democratically elected leaders like Salvador Allende, and others, both abroad and here at home. Too many to count.

Operation Mockingbird was a Cold War–era program aimed at shaping public perception by influencing U.S. news coverage—recruiting journalists, leaning on editors, and working through cutouts and front groups so propaganda could pass as reporting.

Afghanistan wasn't about national security—it was about heroin. Nicaragua wasn't just about communism—it was about selling cocaine to Americans.

The Hudson Institute, a conservative think tank based in Washington, D.C. may not call itself an intelligence outfit, but its world is the same world: former CIA directors on its roster, intelligence-linked figures on its stage, and federal money flowing mainly from the Pentagon. Hudson's transparency page links to its 2024 audit, and that audit says the Department of Defense accounted for 96 percent of Hudson's federal grant-and-contract revenue for the year. Hudson has also publicly featured or affiliated with figures like former CIA director Mike Pompeo, former CIA director James Woolsey, and former CIA director Michael Hayden. That does not prove CIA control. It does show a think tank planted deep inside the American defense and intelligence establishment.

And that world did not stay in Washington. It came to Michigan. During the fight over Proposal 1, when voters were being asked whether sick people should be allowed to use marijuana with a doctor's approval, the old drug-war machinery came rolling in right on schedule. John Walters, the White House drug czar at that time, and current Director of the Hudson Institute showed up in Lansing and the Detroit suburbs to campaign against the measure, condemning medical marijuana right beside the the No Pot Shops army.

So when my world started filling with tanks, rifles, raids, and media coordination, the idea of "something bigger" didn't feel impossible anymore. It started to make sense.

That's when the label in my head changed. We weren't just business owners anymore. We'd been flagged—branded as domestic disruptors, "national security concerns." The kind of names that end up on lists. And once you're in that category, the mission isn't to be fair. The mission is to stop you by discrediting you.

The raids made that clear. If this was about law enforcement, it would've been clean: evidence, charges, court. Instead it was overwhelming force and psychological warfare—homes raided, accounts frozen, people arrested at gunpoint, rifles raised in front of pregnant wives. And eventually it became coordinated across Michigan. To other families.

And the most chilling part—the part you only understand later—is that it wasn't designed to generate convictions. It was designed to crush momentum.

The CIA's modus operandi is always indirect complicity.

Not some faceless agent kicking in my door. The power stays off-stage—like a film director—while other people do the acting. You don't see the hands on the controls, but you feel the set move around you: a phone call here, a memo there, a task force "greenlit," a prosecutor emboldened, a narrative fed to the media. And suddenly your life is a set, and you're the villain in a story you didn't write.

Do I have a single document stamped CIA that proves we were targeted, end-to-end? No. What I had were breadcrumbs—backchannels, lawyers, FOIA returns, discovery evidence, conversations I wasn't supposed to hear—and the breadcrumbs kept circling the same name: Operation Michigan Pot Shops, a federal task force green lit to stop the marijuana industry in Michigan even before it started. It sounded absurd—fake, even—but it kept showing up.

And that's the brutal truth that settled in my chest: legality doesn't protect you when power decides you're the example. The law said we were legal. But the machine didn't respond like we were legal. It responded like we were contagious. Like we had to be quarantined in public.

Why would they care? From my seat, the answer wasn't "weed." It was control.

Control over the narrative—who gets called legitimate and who gets called a criminal.

Control over the marketplace—who gets to operate with legitimacy and who gets forced back into the shadows.

Control over fear—because fear is the oldest tool in the kit, and it works.

In that framework, a clean dispensary with a license is dangerous in a way a street dealer isn't. A licensed storefront is harder to discredit. It attracts community support. It makes the hypocrisy visible. And it invites other people to step forward.

So they didn't just come for the product. They came for the story. They needed villains. Headlines. "Proof." And indirect complicity does its work the same way every time: you make the target feel inevitable. You apply pressure through proxies. You let the locals swing the hammer while someone else decides where it lands.

That's how it felt to me, standing there watching it unfold—two guys trying to help sick people, suddenly treated like national threats. And once that thought takes root, it spreads, because it forces the question I never wanted to ask:

If openness is an American value, why did this feel like secrecy, coordination, and punishment? Why did it feel like I wasn't facing the law—but an agenda dressed up as the law?

14

Weird Science

By 2014, after every previous raid, courtroom ambush, and head-line-grabbing press release failed to break us, the prosecutors in Oakland County tried a new tactic. Words hadn't worked. The voters had spoken. The Michigan Medical Marijuana Act was law. So instead of twisting language, they twisted science.

This time, they weren't coming after Jake and I for conspiracy to distribute marijuana—a charge that had become harder to stick in court against us. Now they had to get creative. And so, led by Oakland County prosecutor Mrs. Cooper, they cooked up something entirely new.

They charged us with conspiracy to distribute synthetic marijuana.

Synthetic marijuana—what the law defines as substances manufac-tured to mimic THC but not derived from the cannabis plant. The law we operated under protected marijuana in its natural botanical form. Synthetic cannabinoids? Still Schedule I. Still illegal. Still prose-cutable.

So now they were claiming that the same flower we sold—grown in dirt, trimmed by hand by local farmers—was actually synthetic. Not because it was. But because it could be. According to their "expert."

At the evidentiary hearing, Mrs. Cooper brought in a chemist from the Michigan State Police crime lab. Andrea Banis. A woman with a white coat, a government badge, legitimacy and a quiet voice.

She took the stand and delivered the line that would define the insanity of this whole ordeal:

"Based on the molecular structure...," she said, "that the cannabis seized is likely synthetic in nature."

She refused to make eye contact with Jake or I, keeping her gaze pinned to the floor and the prosecutor. My grunts and emotions were obvious—filling the courtroom with my non-legal objections. My lawyer leaned in and quietly motioned for me to calm it down.

Not that it was synthetic. Not that it even tested as synthetic. Just that it could be. A theoretical argument. A hypothetical used to justify a felony. Total bullshit.

The judge bought it.

Of course he did. How many judges understand chemistry, or cannabis pharmacology? Especially when the testimony comes from someone in a lab coat who speaks with institutional confidence? To them, science is a black box. And the government controls the input and the output.

I could understand a prosecutor like Mrs. Cooper—already aligned with the No Pot Shops crowd—pulling a stunt like this. That was her lane. But what turned my stomach was watching a medical professional do it. Someone who'd sworn an oath to do no harm, lending her name and credentials to a charade she had to know would hurt real people.

Because the damage didn't just land on me. It landed on the patients—like the chemo patients we were trying to help—people who didn't have time for politics, or posturing, or "messages." They just needed relief. And here was a doctor helping build the very story that made that relief harder to reach

After her testimony, I found Mrs. Banis in the hallway. I confronted her.

"You know this isn't right," I told her. "You're lying against people like me and Jake—people trying to help patients, not harm them."

She didn't deny it. She didn't push back. She looked down at the floor, visibly uncomfortable. "I'm just doing my job," she muttered. "I just want to go home at night."

Just following orders. That old line.

Jake was charged alongside me. We both stood accused of trafficking a product the state now called hypothetically synthetic. A new statute they invented to slow progress. We knew it was bullshit. We'd seen a lot of creative legal arguments over the years, but this was surreal—even for Oakland County.

This attack felt personal, not professional.

I was up against the same prosecutor from my Clinical Relief trial. She'd stacked charges on us before—charges that never stuck. And now she seemed willing to try anything, throw anything, just to make one of them finally land.

Our response was always the same.

We didn't take pleas. We didn't fold. We took it as personally as they did.

And, yeah—we didn't want to go to jail.

Eventually, the charges were dropped. Bound over for trial, yes—but dismissed before we ever made it to a jury. Because even the prosecutors knew the case had no legs. Not in science. Not in law. Not in anything resembling truth.

Turns out, what happened to Jake and me wasn't an isolated miscarriage of justice—it was part of a pattern. A deliberate one. By 2015, the truth started to trickle out in the press. The Detroit News ran a headline that sounded familiar to me: "State Police Labs Face Scrutiny Over Drug Test Accuracy." The very lab that had labeled our cannabis "possibly synthetic" was under fire for doing the same thing to others—hundreds of others. Maybe thousands.

Whistleblowers inside the Michigan State Police crime lab had revealed that prosecutors across the state, especially in Oakland county, were actively pressuring forensic scientists, like Andrea, to misreport results. Label it synthetic even if you knew it wasn't. The goal? Upgrade legal marijuana possession and sales to felonies.

The internal communications between lab analysts and prosecutors were damning. One email chain showed a senior MSP official instructing staff to classify certain marijuana samples as Schedule I synthetic analogues—even when no such substances were found.

Most defendants didn't have the money, time, or stomach to fight back. Plea deals were taken. Records were stained. Lives were upended. Children removed from homes. And all the while, the public was fed a narrative about rogue dispensaries and dangerous drugs—when in reality, the real danger was happening inside the walls of the state's own forensic labs.

What I remember most from that trial isn't the fear or frustration. It's watching my criminal defense attorney, Neil, go toe-to-toe with their experts—not with emotion or spin, but with actual science. He came into that courtroom with stacks of medical journals and peer-reviewed studies. He spoke the language of the chemist. He challenged their conclusions point by point.

He knew the material as well as Mrs. Banis did. Maybe better.

In one court filing Neil wrote: As an aficionado of "good lawyering," undersigned counsel admired the [Prosecutor's] pleading paper. However, as an advocate, undersigned counsel could not let pass the observation that the government went to much effort, with many alternatives, twists, turns and creativity....

But it didn't matter. Not to the judge. In the courtroom, the prosecutor and the prosecution's expert always carries more weight—no matter how flawed, no matter how ridiculous.

That's when I realized: in this fight, facts aren't enough.

You have to outlast the lies

THE MICHIGAN STATE POLICE Forensic Science Division finds itself embroiled in scandal as newly released emails paint a picture of a crime lab in turmoil over how to classify marijuana. Attorneys and medical marijuana advocates accuse Michigan prosecutors of pressuring the state's crime lab to falsely classify the origins of THC found in hash oils and marijuana edibles as "origin unknown."

Prosecutors exploited the ambiguity to charge medical marijuana users for possession of synthetic THC, despite the fact that the personal use of medical marijuana has been legal in Michigan since it was approved by voters in 2008. Under Michigan law, possession of synthetic THC constitutes a felony, whereas possession of marijuana and its derivatives by someone who is not a licensed medical marijuana user is a misdemeanor.

Excerpt from a 2015 article published by *The Intercept.*

15

Laughs and Baseball Wins

Not every day in the dispensary trenches was doom and dread. Sure, we were getting raided every month, but between the court dates, asset seizures, and DEA paranoia, we still managed to laugh. A lot. Humor, as it turned out, was a hell of a survival tool.

The dispensary crew—Amanda, Cassie, Trinity, Jake, John, Johnnie, Dan, and the rest—had a way of finding joy in the absurdity of it all. Our stores weren't just a place to pick up meds; they were a stage for characters straight out of a stoner noir sitcom.

Our customers? Outside of the sick, they were a blend of the unbelievable and unforgettable. Like any retail job, we had our regulars, our favorites, and our "Oh God, he's back" types.

There were the creepers who turned every female budtender interaction into a creepy audition for The Bachelor. The strippers—somehow all armed with legitimate medical marijuana cards—who brought an air of perfume and dollar bills to the shop. There were local legends, too: NHL enforcer Darren McCarty lived just minutes away and stopped by occasionally. The great-granddaughter of Henry Ford, who once wrote us a thank-you letter after her best friend used cannabis from our dispensary to cope with chemo.

And then there was Dave—my personal favorite. A multiple sclerosis survivor who had every reason to be bitter, but instead brought the whole room to tears laughing. His visits were reminders that what we were doing mattered.

But the growers? They were a show all their own.

Every guy with a light setup in a basement swore they had "the best shit you've ever seen, bro." Jake managed all the vendor purchases, but one of the perks of working behind the counter was free "samples." Yep—real product from hopeful vendors, just sitting in the break room like potluck desserts for our pot loving staff. Our team would smoke them and give feedback to Jake. Quality control at its finest.

That free cannabis even helped me on occasion to shoulder the stress and keep the train on the tracks—or, at least for a little while, helped me forget the train was under constant attack.

Jake once asked me to join him on a trip to a Lansing grow operation inside an abandoned airplane hangar. Naturally. Because nothing says "legit operation" like surplus World War II real estate.

The grower was a nonstop smoker—paranoid and twitchy from either the weed or the illegality of his operation. Maybe both. When he saw me and Jake's brother Dan with Jake, he panicked.

"Who are they?" he demanded. "I told you to come alone!"

Then he asked to frisk us for wires. Dan wasn't having it. "Fuck no, man," he snapped.

But Dan—being Dan—couldn't leave it there. He leaned into his shirt and muttered, "Perp in possession. Tango Four. That's affirmative…" like he was relaying intel to the feds.

The grower's eyes bulged. "Who are you talking to?!"

Dan deadpanned, "Man, you are way too stoned. Nobody said anything."

"Roger that. Durango out" I whispered into my shirt collar.

We walked out with a hell of a deal—bought at 25% of retail with no counter offer—and weren't invited back. The grower did keep selling to Jake, though. Minus the company.

Other growers came with baggage. One was so obsessed with one of our budtenders—part of the "Ryan's Angels" crew—that he offered to let her and her young daughter move in with him and "his children"–meaning his weed plants. Romance, stoner-style. The courtship consisted mostly of awkward compliments and weekly follow-up deliveries. "Is Trinity working today"?

Let's be honest: back then, the cannabis community was a bizarre cast of misfits unlike the clean cut Wall Street types in charge today. We weren't just the pioneers—we were the pirates. Socially awkward growers who treated plants like children and kept everyone out of their basement grow rooms, veteran pot dealers with pilot licenses who long claimed to be "art dealers," and Deadheads who somehow made it out of the 1970s with decent genetics and full-blown PTSD.

One of our growers was a regular buyer of our Kind Baked edibles—professionally packaged, legit branding, the real deal. His cousin? An athletic trainer for the Cincinnati Reds. Not long after our infused treats started making their way into the clubhouse, half the team was reportedly riding the high.

That same stretch, the Reds made it to the National League Division Series two out of three seasons. Coincidence? We're not convinced.

We weren't just slinging weed.

We were fueling laughter, friendship, pain relief, and—apparently—playoff baseball.

So no, the dispensary days weren't all dark. There were moments of absurd joy, weird science, and enough inside jokes to fill a stand-up routine.

Our Kind Baked food line provided relief and convenience to many patients.

16

Dispensaries That Never Were

Redford and Lincoln Park were different communities, but they played the same role: border towns pressed up against Detroit, like Warren—just outside the line, close enough to benefit from the urban sprawl customer, and close enough to blame Detroit for anything they didn't want to admit existed in their own streets.

And the border cops could be just as aggressive—sometimes worse—because their identity was tied up in keeping Detroit out, along with anything they associated with it, including medical marijuana. They weren't just policing crime; they were policing the line—protecting their residents from "Detroiters," as if a city could be reduced to a type of person.

So when Jake and I showed up—dispensary entrepreneurs from the other side of that cultural border, outsiders—we got filed into the same category: outsiders bringing trouble, bringing "that Detroit stuff," bringing something they didn't understand and didn't want. The irony was we weren't invading. We were opening a business none of their residents had the balls to do—and plenty of their residents needed. The blue-collar working class, the people who'd spent decades on their feet getting ground down in the car factories, riding home sore and exhausted, looking for something that actually helped.

But to them, the border wasn't geography. It was a mindset. And the badge was the gate.

Redford looked safe on paper—suburban, kind of. The kind of place that acted like Detroit's problems stopped at Telegraph Road—the west side's version of Eight Mile—as if the city's gravity respected municipal boundaries.

Jake and I did what we always did when we believed something could work: we invested like we planned to stay.

We paid for a full buildout—real money up front. New carpet. New walls. Floorplan. Fresh paint. Bright lighting that didn't buzz. Glass jewelry cases that made everything look legitimate, like it belonged behind a counter instead of in a Ziploc baggie. We tore out the spaghetti mess of old phone and cable lines stapled through the ceiling from decades of tenants. By the time we were done, we'd improved the landlord's property in ways he never would've paid for himself.

We put Dave in charge of Redford. Jake's brother's best friend. A squirrely guy with a used car salesmen suit and a constant sting of cigarettes. What I didn't know—and what I couldn't recognize until being told—was that Dave was a massive pill popper. I've never been good at spotting it. I miss the tells. I miss the slow unraveling. The beet red face.

After the buildout was complete, we were down to the simplest part—the part that's supposed to be boring. We needed one signoff from the city. Just one. The occupancy permit.

The inspector had a conflict and rescheduled. I had one too—a court hearing for the Ferndale trial—so I didn't go.

The building inspector was scheduled for 2:00 p.m. I told Dave like I was delivering a court order: be there early, be ready, don't do anything stupid.

He couldn't resist lighting one up before the inspector arrived—inside the building. What a jackass.

The inspector smelled the doobie immediately and did what bureaucracy does when it wants to stay out of trouble: he made it someone else's problem. He called the cops. And because the cops were next door—about a half mile away—it escalated fast. Quick, loud, theatrical, like they'd been waiting for a reason to do what they already wanted to do.

Dave didn't get arrested for the half-lit joint. He got arrested for the ounce or three in his car—and they slapped him with intent-to-distribute, like he was running weight. They charged him like he had ten pounds. It was Redford's way of shutting down a store that was about to open in their town before the first sale was ever made.

Redford never opened. It didn't even get the dignity of a short run. We poured tens of thousands into a store that never saw a single normal day of business—a clean showroom built for legitimacy that got treated like a crime scene before it ever got to be a store.

And because lawyers and legal paper cost more than carpenters and nails, we didn't just lose the buildout money—we got nailed twice as hard financially.

And because I thought transparency still counted for something, I called the township supervisor—what people lazily call "the mayor," because township government doesn't fit neatly in anyone's head unless they've sat through enough boring government meetings like I had.

She was polite. Professional. The kind of woman who didn't raise her voice because she didn't need to. I told her we planned to open, reminded her that plenty of her 'black-and blue-collar' residents needed what we offered, and asked—carefully—whether she could assure me there wouldn't be another problem.

She told me she was "just doing her job," and I heard what she didn't say: I don't want to get in conflict with my police department over a dispensary from out of towners.

For a while I blamed Dave—because you have to blame someone, and the obvious culprit is comforting. But the deeper lesson was uglier: even if you build it clean, even if you do everything right, the outcome is still controlled by people who already want you gone.

I'd put my faith and trust in someone else. I picked the wrong guy. Jake's parents picked the wrong guy to live next to, and Jake's brother picked the wrong dude to befriend. I hadn't handled the last detail. I blamed myself and apologized to Jake.

In Redford, a smell was enough. And I should've smelled Dave before he ever came to us.

By then Jake had uncovered the theft too—cash and product not lining up, numbers that kept drifting, the same shifty story every time you asked. And then Jake finally told me the truth about Dave's drug use.

"What the fuck, Jake?" I said. "Why wouldn't you tell me this before?"

I didn't wait for an answer. I told Jake I'd fire Dave. It was my fault, and I'd handle it. Jake had hired him, but I let him go. Jake still had to deal with his brother, so I got to play the bad guy.

That's what set off World War III.

Dave didn't take responsibility. He rewrote the story. In his version, we weren't two guys cleaning up after his mistakes—we were the reason his life was a mess. Every problem he'd created suddenly belonged to us. And once he decided that, he treated retaliation like a job.

He started calling the cops on us—local departments, Warren cops, our lawyers demanding payouts, anyone he thought might listen. The irony was, some of the Warren officers were decent, and one of them called me with the kind of half-laugh you only hear from someone who's seen every kind of human mess.

"You must've pissed this guy off something good," he said.

Then came the threats. Voicemails. Emails. The same lines repeated like a script he'd memorized: I'll tell law enforcement. The feds. I'll call the IRS on you. I'll make your life hell. Give me some money.

He was trying to extort us the day after we fired him—like we owed him severance for his own opioid addiction. He wanted money, not rehab. Money for his marital problems, his foreclosed home, his foreclosed life. And when we didn't pay, he escalated, because that's what desperate people do when they've run out of leverage: they weaponize whatever institutions they think will hurt you the most.

Jake and I were eventually forced to file for a restraining order against him.

After the federal charges came down against me a decade later, he resurfaced to taunt me again—like my life was responsible for his rotten one. Like my downfall was his way of rewriting the past and laundering his guilt and addiction and failures into something that looked like justice.

One text message on my cellphone read: You piece of shit. I hope you rot in a jail. Karma is a mother.

Less than a week later, Dave died of a massive heart attack.

Unlike Dave, the Lincoln Park dispensary at least got to breathe for a while.

Lincoln Park sits on Detroit's southern border. Down there the dividing line isn't Eight Mile—it's Outer Drive. And the cops protected that line the same way the other suburban border guards did: like their job was less about policing crime and more about keeping "Detroit" from crossing over.

It stayed open for several months—long enough to feel real, long enough for routines to form and managers to be anointed, long enough for patients to become familiar and make repeat purchases—long enough, even, that we issued loyalty cards like we were any other friendly neighborhood pharmacy.

Our dispensary sat across from two legitimate national pharmacy chains—drug stores with fluorescent aisles full of profit, addiction, and corporate respectability. Nobody acted offended by drugs there, because those drugs came in amber bottles and carried the blessing of the system.

We put the same money into Lincoln Park that we'd put into Redford—maybe more. Another full buildout. Another clean retail footprint. Another row of glass cases. Another landlord's property improved on our dime because we kept believing professionalism would function as armor.

Then the elections hit, and with them came the new mayor—one of those quiet political weather changes that doesn't look like a storm until you're already standing in the rain. My lawyer emailed me after making calls—after the police harassment and intimidation began. He'd spoken with the City Attorney, who might be willing to meet, but he was already hedging. He mentioned "issues" with the recent election and the new mayor, and suggested—almost casually—that a neighboring community might be more beneficial now that the politicians had changed.

Legalese for Detroit.

That's when the raids got harsher. One, then two, then the big one. Each time, a little louder. A little more confident—like the force had to be nudged at first, then trained, and eventually turned loose.

And underneath all of it was the same message, delivered with force:

You are not welcome.

Two of our staff were hauled off in the last raid—John, a Sammy Hagar lookalike with a musician's smile and a caregiver's pride, and Cassie, one of Ryan's Angels.

They weren't criminals in any honest sense. They were political prisoners—caged for the same reason many of us had been, and for the same reason plenty before us were: the rules were still being written by men with badges and grudges.

There's an old saying—always credited to the people who benefit from it—that goes something like: you make the laws, I'll make the rules, and I'll win every time.

Even in okay towns like Lincoln Park, it only takes one bad apple to spoil the whole lot. There was one officer who took extreme pride in being a real dickhead—smashing cabinets, lecturing patients and staff, and making sure everyone heard it: you "don't want to fuck around here."

Lincoln Park lasted longer than Redford, but it never stood a chance either. The decision wasn't made after we opened. It was made before we were fully understood.

I wrote the judge—not because I thought it would help, but because it felt like the only thing left to do. As it turned out, it did.

Your Honor,

Without the moral panic surrounding medical marijuana, you likely would never have met Cassandra or John. I understand you are fully aware of the facts and the backdrop, so I won't dance around it: this situation is unfair. These are good people, and it's a hard thing to watch their futures placed in anyone's hands but their own.

I'm told you are a fair and reasoned judge, and I believe you can see the absurdity here—an absurdity that, candidly, even the prosecutor seems to recognize. Regardless, given the circumstances, this path appeared to be the best option in John and Cassandra's interests.

Over the past year and a half, I've had the opportunity to work closely with both of them. They are dependable, thoughtful, and exercise good judgment—qualities that matter in any profession, but especially in an industry that many choose to label "dangerous" simply because it is misunderstood. They are productive members of society who make careful decisions and take the law seriously.

Cassandra has no meaningful history, and while John's record may have affected his financial stability, it does not define his character. Both John and Cassandra contribute to their families and their community, and I hope the Court sees them for who they are, not for the assumptions others attach to this work.

I also want to be clear about something Lincoln Park PD—and much of society—seems unwilling to accept: when John and Cassandra say they are caregivers, they mean it. They say it proudly because they believe in what they do. Yes, there are people who hide behind that label for the wrong reasons. Cassandra and John are not those people.

If the Court would like any additional information regarding their character or my experience working with them, I am available and can be reached by phone 248-###-####.

Respectfully,

Ryan Richmond

The charges were eventually dropped. As a kind of peace offering, they were left with a small fine and "time served" for the two days they'd already spent in jail. They went right back to work the next day.

* * *

Redford and Lincoln Park were different only in timing.

Redford never got off the ground because one employee couldn't follow the simplest instructions—and because putting a dispensary next to a police station doesn't make you safer. It makes you easier.

Lincoln Park stayed open longer, sat across from legitimate pharmacies, and still got told to leave. Because the point was never the details. Not the buildout. Not the location. Not the neighbors. Not the patients.

The point was that Jake and I had crossed an invisible border and set up shop in a place that defined itself by what it kept out. To them, we weren't entrepreneurs. We weren't caregivers. We were a breach.

And in those years—and even in these years, right now—that was enough.

The front door of our Relief Choices location in Lincoln Park. None of our stores had signage out front—part security design, part discretion for our patients.

17

I Smell Pot

Cousin Gary had been hinting for about a year that he wanted to make some extra money, asking how he could get involved. I wanted to help him more than anything, but I kept reminding him, "Gary—I've never even seen you smoke pot before. What would you even do?"

He didn't care. He wanted in.

Then he showed up with a plan. He told me and Jake he could grow cannabis in a rental house his father-in-law owned and then sell it to us. What did we have to lose? We even handed him grow lights and equipment left over from our now out-of-commission Rochester Hills facility. We were genuinely happy to help him get started.

Jake became the buyer—and to keep Gary afloat, he paid above market for what was, honestly, a sub-par harvest.

A few months after the operation got going, I went to visit Gary at the grow house in downtown Holly. The second I pulled up, my first thought was: this is going to draw heat.

It was obvious. Too close to the neighbors. Too cozy with the neighbors. And the smell—nothing about it was properly contained. It drifted through the neighborhood like a signal flare. The air scrubbers we'd given him were still sitting there, unused in the box.

Worse, Gary was standing there drinking beer in the driveway with two hillbilly neighbors posted up next to their pickup trucks, talking like this was backyard gardening.

I pulled him aside. "Gary—you can't be talking about this. You can't be letting people know."

I wasn't just worried for him. I was worried for me. By then I'd watched cops bust hundreds of grows—even "legal" ones like Gary's. The routine was always the same: raid, arrest, hire a lawyer, then stand in front of a judge and prove you were compliant after the fact. Once you're on their radar, the details become an afterthought.

Gary waved it off. "Everything will be alright," he said. "They're cool."

Sure enough, word of Gary's grow made its way to the county narcotics team. And one of those officers was Doty—who was now part of the drug team working under Sheriff Bouchard.

Once word came down that an investigation had started—and that a raid was scheduled for the grow house, a property and operation Doty knew all about—he called Gary in a panic.

"You've got one day," he warned. "They're going to hit the house. Get everything out—now."

It wasn't the first time Doty bailed Gary out. A few months earlier, paperwork with Gary's name on it—tied to a raid at a Pontiac dispensary he was supplying—somehow "got corrected." Doty made sure it vanished. That shop sat in a failed bank branch, the kind with a steel vault in the back and pneumatic tubes still bolted to the ceiling. Drive-through windows sold convenience: pot with curbside pickup. Honestly, the property was perfect—secure, high-visibility, plenty of parking. But at that moment, Pontiac was ground zero for the No Pot Shops brigade.

When the raid came, it was textbook—lights, rifles, evidence bags, press calls. Names of owners and suppliers got listed. Then, quietly, one of those names didn't. Gary's. We even got the insider's cut. Afterward, Gary showed me and Jake a video Doty shot from inside the operation—his own phone camera footage, recorded mid-raid.

Now Gary needed our help again. He called Jake.

"Jake, I've got almost 100 plants I need to move. I can't afford to lose them."

Jake, always the fixer, agreed. He offered up an old warehouse that we used to store supplies and where Jake would sometimes work out of. Gary made about five trips in his minivan, hauling the plants forty minutes each way.

On his final trip, undercover officers tailed him. As Gary stepped out of the building, the drug team closed in—guns drawn—and cuffed him right there on the spot.

Shortly after, I drove by the Hazel Park warehouse and saw the place crawling with police cars. I tried calling Gary. Nothing. His minivan was in the lot, which told me he was inside—but I had no idea what was happening in there until later.

I called Jake immediately.

"Jake—they got Gary."

Jake rushed over. Braver, and maybe more foolish in that moment than I was.

Inside, officers were bagging and tagging Gary's plants as evidence, moving through the warehouse like they owned it—pulling, photographing, inventorying, taking their time.

Jake walked up like he belonged there.

"What is going on here?" he asked one of the officers. "Who are you, and what are you doing in this building?" the officer replied.

Jake told them, "I'm renting the building." Which wasn't a lie. Jake's name and not the business name was on the lease.

Jake paused. Looked around at the rows of plants, the operation laid open like a carcass.

"So all this is yours?" they asked.

Silence.

In that moment, Jake realized his visit wasn't helping Gary—and it wasn't helping Jake. He was just standing in a crime scene, volunteering himself to be remembered.

"Am I free to go?" he asked.

They took his ID anyway. Ran it. Logged it into their notepad. Then let him walk back out into the daylight.

Meanwhile, in the back of a blacked-out narcotics SUV, Gary pleaded his case: "My best friend is Doty." One of the officers called Doty from his personal cell phone. Gary was handed the phone.

"Shut the fuck up!" Doty barked. "Don't say anything until I get there."

And just like that, Gary disappeared from the equation. Doty swept the scene, again, scrubbing Gary's name from every detail. He was recast as a bystander, just a guy passing by a warehouse.

Those 100 plants? They weren't Gary's anymore. They were mine and Jake's.

It was just one more in a long list of lies from Doty—another small pledge of allegiance from a foot soldier in the No Pot Shops crusade, offered up this time for his best friend.

What followed was a full-scale operation—task forces and local law enforcement raiding multiple counties. They hit my house, Jake's home, two of my rentals, my office, and our Warren dispensary.

Sarah was walking around with two brand new hips and was pregnant at the time—something I didn't fully process until later. Assault rifles were leveled at my front door, and then at her forehead, as they forced their way into our home while we sat on the couch watching a movie.

They ransacked the house. Then they marched me outside and put me in the back of one of the seven marked patrol cars parked out front, while the neighbors watched through their window shades—another raid, another public humiliation.

Police reports described Jake as "very obese." Even so, they dragged him out of his home, cuffed his hands behind his back, and left him sitting for hours in the back of a patrol car—something that wasn't standard procedure for someone his size. By the time his wrists flared up with tendinitis, they finally transported him to the county jail and put him in a cell next to mine.

For two days, we said very little. We assumed we were being recorded. But mostly, we were just exhausted.

Somehow, Jake came out of it even more determined—refocused. He wanted to expand operations, hire more staff, keep building. And he was mad. Not just angry at what they'd done to us, but furious in a deeper way—more fired up than all the other abuses we'd already taken.

I was done. Things were different now. I started preparing my exit.

Sarah had a front-row seat to the absurdity—the politics—that came with every raid before this one. And as usual, she stood by me. She always did.

But I didn't want my unborn son to enter a world where police raids were normal. Where a knock at the door—or a convoy in a parking lot—was just another part of doing business.

* * *

Once released, we both tried to reach Gary. We were now looking at 25-year charges—for Gary's plants.

But Gary went dark.

A week later, on a cold November afternoon, I pulled up to Gary's place. He was outside with the garage door open, lingering like he'd been waiting on bad news all day. I walked right up to him.

"Gary," I said, "we're in deep. I'm not blaming you. I just need you to talk to my lawyer, Neil. We walk away alive from this—we know what we're doing. We're not scared."

But Doty had gotten to him first. Doty had told him to stay silent. Say nothing. Especially not to us.

Gary's voice was small when he answered. He said he was scared. That my lawyer would protect me and not him. He said he didn't want anything bad to happen to his family. I told him I wanted the same thing—for him and for us. That this wasn't about throwing anyone under a bus. It was about getting the facts straight before the system wrote its own version.

It was obvious what he believed: if the truth came out, he would be the one left holding it—Gary, alone—while Jake and I found a way to pay lawyers to get us out of it. He saw himself as the actual defendant and me as the prosecutor.

But after watching raid after raid go sideways—cops getting sloppy, reports turning elastic, lies getting uncovered—I'd learned something: charges get dropped for all.

Gary didn't respond. Not to me. But he did agree to talk to Neil.

In that call, which Neil played for me later, Gary admitted everything. Doty had warned him. Doty had saved him. And at the end of the conversation, Gary made it clear:

"I will not testify. I will not harm Doty."

Neil pressed him. "Your cousin is facing some serious time. Are you sure?"

Neil's advice was cold but honest: "Doty will be fine. Nothing ever happens to cops. I've been doing this a long time."

Gary had made his choice.

He would protect Doty—not me, not Jake.

He didn't know the call was recorded. But he didn't need to. Lawyers can legally record as part of their investigation. And Neil had everything he needed.

We didn't need Gary to testify. He already had.

Just like the raids before, officers drained my bank accounts again—money not even tied to marijuana—while Neil and I debated whether to take the recording to the prosecutor.

"Why don't we just play it for them?" I asked. "Stop the bleeding."

"We wait," Neil said. "Preliminary hearing first."

When the hearing came, officers swore under oath: "We smelled pot outside the warehouse as we drove by."

Not that Doty tipped off Gary. Not that they tailed Gary. Not that they watched him move 100 plants. Just that often used lie during marijuana arrests: "We smelled pot."

Neil went to work, grilling them about their reports. The inconsistencies. The matching falsehoods. The perjury.

And then he dropped the letter to the prosecutor.

The letter wasn't a complaint. It was a map. Names. Dates. Addresses. A timeline that didn't care about their sworn bedtime story. He addressed it to the top of NET—Sgt. Stewart—and to Doty himself, like he wanted them to feel the envelope in their hands before anyone else did.

He laid out what we were saying had really happened. Not "we smelled pot," but why they were at that warehouse in the first place. Neil described Doty investigating a dispensary in Pontiac—Sky High—then recording the raid on his phone like it was a souvenir. And then, according to what Neil had learned, Doty met up with Gary and showed him that raid video, casually, like you'd show a buddy a clip from a game.

The letter made one simple argument: if the investigation was built on misconduct, then everything that came after it was rotten. The Hazel Park warrant. The seizure. The "evidence." The whole neat little narrative about smelling marijuana as they drove by. Neil wasn't asking for favors—he was putting NET on notice and daring them to deny it. Return what was taken. Open an internal inquiry. Explain to a prosecutor—on paper—how a narcotics detective ends up helping his best friend while men like me and Jake get the full weight of the state dropped on our necks.

That's what Neil slid across the table. Not emotion. Not outrage. A document that forced everyone to pick a side: either the system was going to pretend this was normal, or it was going to admit the truth—that the raids weren't about law enforcement, they were about power. And power protects its own.

The charges were dropped. Jake and I walked free. Just like I told Gary would happen.

Neil had told Gary: nothing would happen to Doty.

And he was right.

The money was never returned. Asset forfeiture swallowed it whole, again.

I would eventually learn later, through family and friends of Gary, that he blamed me for recording the call, as if I'd driven a knife straight into the heart of our relationship. In that instant, the trust we'd built over a lifetime split clean down the middle—and it never came back. It wouldn't be the last time Gary stood on the sidelines when I needed him most. Maybe the adult bullies were just too much for him, harder and meaner than the ones we faced in the old neighborhood.

I was gutted. We'd been through so much together, and in my mind, he'd always been the bigger, tougher brother. But in his own way, Gary had already taught me something important when we were kids—how to take a punch. Without knowing it, he'd been preparing me for the abuses that would come later in life—the kind you never see coming, the kind delivered not by kids, but by men with badges, suits, and government letterhead.

The betrayal cut deep, but it also left me harder, sharper. Maybe that was Gary's final lesson: even the people you'd bet your life on can disappear when the stakes rise high enough.

It also wouldn't be the last time Doty took the stand to lie about me either.

Racism Meets Medical Marijuana

It was the winter of 2014. We were barely past the "I smell pot" incident when another knock came.

This raid wasn't just a threat, or a shakedown, or another "smash your display cabinets" hit with no charges that followed. This one was sanctioned—the kind of raid that comes with paperwork, signatures, and men who believe that makes it righteous. By the book. It would be my last raid as an owner in the industry—but it wouldn't be my last raid.

By sunrise, Jake and I were wiped out. Our corporate and personal bank accounts were cleared—zeroed like someone hit reset.

This wasn't some smash-and-grab robbery.

It was a seize-and-take. We went to jail for a couple days—again—but no criminal charges followed.

They didn't need a trial. They didn't need charges. All it took was a judge's signature and the most efficient weapon the drug war ever created: civil asset forfeiture.

That's the part most common people don't understand until it happens to them. Asset forfeiture flips the whole idea of justice on its head. Instead of the government having to prove you did something wrong, they treat your property like it's guilty—your cash, your car, your bank account—then they take it first and ask questions later... if they ask at all.

In a forfeiture case, it's not even you on the caption like a normal prosecution. The case can literally read like: State of Michigan v. $100,000—as if the money did the crime. As if the cash or bank account had intent. As if your bank account woke up one morning and decided to allegedly traffic pot.

And because it's civil, not criminal, the protections people assume you have in court don't show up the same way. No requirement of a conviction. Often not even an arrest. The burden shifts, the process gets murky, and you're left trying to claw back what was yours while the government sits on your lifeline. Bills still come due. Payroll doesn't pause. Lawyers cost money—money they just took.

That's why it works. It's punishment without the sentence.

With a badge and a bank routing number, they took everything we'd built—overnight.

Years of hard work and risk beyond imagination. Gone in hours.

That was the playbook. Starve the business. Bleed the owners. Make it impossible to fight back.

And they were good at it.

Behind this particular raid? Macomb County Prosecutor Eric Smith and the State Attorney General. Smith didn't lead raids; he authorized them. He didn't just carry a gun; he carried a pen. And with that pen, he turned our livelihoods into his personal asset fund again and again.

Smith was more than a prosecutor. He was a corporate raider.

But this raid was different. It had something none of the others did. Something worse. Something I've kept quiet from the world because of what the world might do to me if it found out.

A video.

Three minutes. That's all.

A few days after the raid—after she was released without charges during the raid—one of the Angels told me she'd overheard the cops talking in another room while they were waiting to take her to jail. She was the last one they escorted out.

Her story sounded unreal. But in the middle of their overtime-paid raid, they forgot one thing—just one computer. The one that held the security camera storage.

I asked Jake's brother, Dan, to take a look and see if he could pull everything off it—video, audio, whatever it had.

I took the thumb drive back to my office, slid it into my laptop, and just sat there—staring like the screen was going to blink first.

The internet and home televisions were loaded with videos that had already scorched their way across the country that year—Eric Garner, Michael Brown, Tamir Rice. The country had already watched Black men die at the hands of law enforcement—footage that lingered. Their deaths were horrific, and I won't pretend there's a scale for that. But what I was about to watch was a different kind of brutality., and I'm not pretending there's a "worse" than that.

Because death on video is blunt-force trauma. It's violence you can point to. You can name it. You can mourn it. You can rage at it.

This was something else: words—used like a weapon. Not shouted in the heat of chaos, but delivered with that calm confidence that only comes from a man who believes the room, the city belongs to him. And hearing it—especially from a white cop—felt like watching the mask come off in real time.

Three minutes of footage—captured inside our Warren dispensary—framed at an angle so clean it felt staged, like Spielberg himself had picked the spot and called "action." In those three minutes, everything became clear: what this was about, who we were to them, and why they kept coming back.

On that tape, one of the officers from the Warren Police Department in front of fellow officers, brass from the Macomb County Sheriff's Office, and members of COMET (a DEA-backed narcotics task force) could be heard saying things no person in uniform — no person at all — should ever say.

"I hate niggers. Niggers love weed. This place brings niggers to us."

It wasn't just one remark, or one bad slur. It was a tirade. A casual, open spillage of hatred from the mouth of the government sworn to serve and protect. The kind of language that would have made even Hillbilly Hitler flinch.

This wasn't random prejudice. This was policy for departments north of 8 Mile Road, west of Telegraph Road and south of Outer Drive. Keeping the line of us and them. Black and white.

Eric Garner's fatal arrest was caught on camera by Ramsey Orta that summer—the kind of footage that doesn't just show something, it stains the country with it. Orta filmed as NYPD officer Daniel Pantaleo put Garner in a chokehold over something as small and stupid as selling loose cigarettes. And Garner's voice kept cutting through the noise—"I can't breathe"—until it didn't.

The video detonated across the nation, sparked protests, and forced people to stare at what they'd been trained to look past. But Orta paid for being the witness. Not long after, his own life got dragged into courtrooms—guns, drugs—and he said the police made him a target afterward, like the punishment wasn't for what he did, but for what he recorded. He never said he regretted filming it. He said he regretted not staying anonymous.

I couldn't remain anonymous—even if I wanted to—because releasing that video would put a spotlight on what black metro Detroit residents had been saying for years, and what even the feds already knew about the department. I was afraid. Still am if I am being honest.

Warren, Michigan — the state's third-largest city — had no Black police officers. The Department of Justice had sued the city twice over its failure to hire black officers. Both times, Warren denied there was a problem.

It wasn't until a black woman named Officer DeSheila Howlett was hired that the number went from zero to one. And even she would become a target.

Howlett would later file a federal lawsuit against the city, alleging years of racial discrimination on the force. She recounted being denied backup at crime scenes, being slurred by fellow officers, and enduring some particularly vicious remarks from her own partner:

"You look like the Gorilla Glue gorilla."

"My Slave Girl"

That partner was Detective Johnson—the same guy who participated in several of the raids on our business and showed up on the day of the "n-word video" raid. Same man who befriended Jake and then slapped cuffs on him like it was all part of the plan.

The same guy staff watched take cash from our register and slide it into his pocket—no inventory count, no evidence bag, no receipt. Just gone, like the rules didn't apply to him because he was the one enforcing them.

From my viewpoint he wasn't all bad. Years later, Johnson helped me at trial—when he testified, truthfully and on the record.

Our security cam footage could have strengthened De Sheila's case, proven that the racism she endured was not imagined, not isolated, but systemic. But I couldn't share it. Not then. Not when the price might have been my life.

Because after that raid, and after using it as a bargaining chip, everything escalated.

My home was broken into. My office ransacked. Computers destroyed, files stolen, cameras turned away from where they should have been pointing. They weren't looking for cash and bank accounts. They were now looking for the video.

At first, I chalked it up to paranoia — a hazard of the business. But then came the warning.

"There are people who would kill you over that video," someone close to law enforcement told me. "You should forget you ever saw it."

I couldn't forget. But I also couldn't risk my family's safety.

A few days after the raid, I paid a visit to Detective Rushton, Warren's lead narcotics officer. I sat across from him in his office, my bank accounts frozen, my life in shambles.

"Do your people always talk like this?" I asked. "Do they always despise minorities?"

"What do you mean?" he said, forcing a nervous smile.

"I saw the tape," I told him. "Do you think we don't have cameras in there?"

He knew exactly what I meant, but he looked tired—not angry, just worn down.

"I just want to go home to my kids," he said quietly, like a man resigned to a system he couldn't fix. His compromise was simple: "You be cool, we'll be cool."

"Will you return my money?" I asked.

He didn't answer. He didn't have to. A few weeks later, a check arrived. Just $30,000 — a fraction of what they'd taken. In all, I'd lost over $150,000 in that raid.

Shortly after the money came back, I retired from the cannabis industry. I handed it all to Jake—everything. The patients, the equipment, even the Angels. I'd had enough.

* * *

Years later, the mask finally slipped.

In March 2020, Eric Smith resigned amid allegations that he had misused roughly $600,000 from drug forfeiture accounts—the accounts he filled when he drained our bank accounts and cash registers. The cash skipped the banking process entirely.

A Michigan State Police investigation, later joined by the FBI, revealed that Smith had been running secret, unauthorized accounts for public funds for years.

In April 2020, he was charged with 10 felonies, including embezzlement, official misconduct, and conspiracy. In January 2021, Smith pleaded guilty in federal court to obstruction of justice for interfering with witnesses. A month later, my soon-to-be federal judge—Linda Parker—sentenced him to 21 months in prison. Less time than she'd eventually give me.

But the reckoning didn't end there. In September 2023, Smith was convicted on three additional state felony counts—official misconduct, evidence tampering, and forgery—and sentenced to a year in state prison, plus probation, community service, restitution, and forfeiture of his pension.

Smith, the man who once wielded a pen like a weapon, would now spend his nights behind bars.

Desheila eventually settled her federal lawsuit for an undisclosed sum. The City of Warren paid out with taxpayer money—no apology, no admission of wrongdoing.

Nothing to see here. Move on.

But don't worry—Mr. Smith wasn't all bad. He was part of the No Pot Shops committee, just "protecting the kids," shoulder to shoulder with Sheriff Bouchard, Attorney General Schuette, the Macomb County Sheriff, and plenty of other public servants who loved the spotlight and hated the plant.

* * *

What happened to us wasn't just about marijuana. It was about control. About race. About power.

The war on cannabis was never really about cannabis. To understand it, you have to go back to 1937, when Congress passed the Marihuana Tax Act. It wasn't science that drove the ban—it was hatred. Henry Anslinger, the first commissioner of the Federal Bureau of Narcotics, called marijuana the "Black man's drug." He claimed it made jazz musicians insane and Mexicans violent.

In the 1930s, the federal government didn't so much "rename" cannabis as choose its weaponized nickname. The plant had long been known in medicine and industry as cannabis (or hemp), but when

Washington moved to criminalize it, the paperwork suddenly leaned hard into "marihuana"—the spelling used in federal statutes.

That word came out of Mexican Spanish, and Harry Anslinger's crusade helped popularize it in the press and politics at exactly the moment anti-immigrant, racial panic was useful fuel. The goal wasn't clarity; it was association—link the drug to "outsiders," to crime, to fear—so "cannabis" the medicine became "marihuana" the menace.

"Reefer makes darkies think they're as good as white men," Anslinger once told reporters.

That was the foundation. That was the playbook.

And in 2014, the machine was still running—just in different uniforms. Warren didn't need cross-burnings or white hoods. They had raids, badges, and asset forfeiture. Racism with a bank account.

We weren't just targeted because we were legitimate. We were targeted because our business disrupted a structure built to criminalize Black and brown communities, seize their property, and keep them under control. Legal marijuana threatened that balance. So they struck back.

* * *

About a year after our cameras caught the racism, a Detroit reporter called me—right around the time Desheila's lawsuit was filed.

"Ryan, I heard you have a video. I'm writing a piece on racism and abuse inside the city of Warren's government."

I said nothing and let him do the talking.

Even though I knew he—and the rest of the media—had played a role in delegitimizing our industry, I still wanted to tell him everything. I wanted him to know what they really thought about the black community. I wanted to ask for his email and send the video right then and there.

I wanted to know how he'd even heard about the video. Was it one of the lawyers—running their mouths like always? It wasn't staff. Not Jake. And it sure as hell wasn't me.

More questions came. I stayed silent.

"No comment." Click.

Then came the inspection notice for a rental property I owned in Warren. It seemed odd, and too random. I showed up anyway. The house was spotless. The tenant—a young mom named Chantel—was there with her mother and toddler. But no inspector ever came.

After twenty minutes, I headed back to my car. That's when I saw a man in khaki pants, polo shirt, high-and-tight haircut, a cellphone clipped to his hip.

"You Ryan?" he asked.

"Yep."

"You got videos. Ones that don't belong anywhere. Why're you talking to the media?"

His tone was accusatory. "Why are you even speaking to people?" he pressed.

I didn't answer. Neil's voice rang in my head: Shut the fuck up.

He leaned in like he was about to share a secret. Eyes locked on mine. He paused—just long enough to make sure it landed—then said, "You know people go missing all the time. And people always believe the police."

I froze. I'd already stood eye-to-eye with SWAT teams, stared down rifles, and endured courtroom prosecutors. But this wasn't the law doing its job. This was personal. A direct verbal threat.

"Why don't you just stay on your side of town?" he added—either trying to soften the threat, or reminding me again I wasn't wanted.

Then he turned and walked off. I didn't see which direction he went—he could've been parked right next to me. I just sat in my car, blank, trying to process what I'd just heard.

I was just a landlord. No longer in the weed business, just managing a property. But apparently, even that was too much.

A few months later, the message got louder. That same rental home—fully paid off—was foreclosed for "nonpayment of property tax." I'd sent the payments in. All of them. The last check had come back weeks earlier, returned like a bad check, stamped as if I'd never tried at all. The county treasurer's office made the money vanish, the paper trail evaporate. And just like that, I lost a property I owned outright.

The funny thing about that county treasurer? He would end up becoming an aide for Eric Smith. Later on, he pleaded guilty to a 90-day misdemeanor—a public official refusing or neglecting to account for county money—in exchange for testifying against him.

By then, I had been fully out of the dispensary business for over a year. I wasn't slinging weed, I wasn't skipping property taxes. I was trying to stay above water. But the city of Warren with the help of the County had already made its decision. The county prosecutor and the treasurer—both later convicted in corruption cases — made sure of it.

* * *

Years later, I would find myself standing in a federal courtroom, staring at the same judge, a black woman who had sentenced Eric Smith to prison for stealing from public money—Judge Linda Parker—as she prepared to sentence me.

The very same judge that sent Hansberry and Watson to prison for robbing me and other drug dealers. The irony was suffocating.

Smith emptied my accounts and abused forfeiture, along with public trust. In the end, he went to prison—sentenced to less time than I got. Even so, the same judge now ordered me to pay federal taxes and penalties on funds taken by the same men she'd already sent away.

They went to prison for taking it. I went to prison for not paying taxes on money I never had—money they'd already spent.

In that moment, I understood the drug war's final evolution: when they can't kick in your door anymore, and they can't delegitimize you, they call the tax man for backup.

19

My Final Dispensary Raid

It was around 10:00 a.m. on a cold Sunday in March 2015 when I pulled into the parking lot of Relief Choices, a place I once co-owned, now merely a closed chapter in my life, or so I thought. On this particular day, I was not an entrepreneur, not a pioneer of Michigan's fledgling medical marijuana movement—I was just a customer. A civilian. A man picking up a weekend bag of sativa.

By then, there had been too many raids. No money left. The juice just wasn't worth the squeeze anymore.

The images still came back uninvited: rifles in my face, agents yelling, Sarah pinned to the wall with a high powered assault rifle aimed at her head—again. Prosecutors twisting science until it was unrecognizable, cops in tactical gear acting like they'd just taken down a cartel.

The accounts, the patient records, the email, the equipment, the lease, the payroll—I had surrendered my share of the business to Jake. I was no longer a boss. And yet, I was still welcomed into the back, into the unspoken inner sanctum of the dispensary.

We talked like co-workers do. Petty gossip. Personal updates. Things I had never been privy to before as owner, now just one of the guys.

By 10:15, my presence had become a distraction. The lobby was filling with anxious patients who needed their medicine. I made my exit as swiftly as I had entered. The dispensary was part of a small strip

116

mall—three other businesses, a two-row parking lot. I had activated the turn signal towards Dequindre Road when I saw them: a swarm of men in ski masks, sprinting toward me, weapons drawn.

I knew what this was. Even if I no longer had ownership, I had lived this moment enough to recognize it. I didn't run. I couldn't. Within seconds, I was dragged from my car and shoved face-down onto the oil-stained pavement. As my cheek hit the ground, I watched one of the masked men dive into my vehicle and park it again.

When they lifted me to my feet, I could finally see it: the dispensary, surrounded. The black-clad men were everywhere, exiting the heating and cooling van parked discreetly nearby—the kind no one notices—now with all its doors ajar. It was an ambush by the so-called Macomb County drug task force, though I would argue "robbery crew" was a more fitting term.

I told them nothing, per Neil's lasting advice.

I was handcuffed, then felt up and down by dirty, racist hands—men who'd been asserting their power over me for years, and over anyone they decided was "undesirable" in their town. I was marched toward the open door of the dispensary I'd started and then cut loose, forced back inside a place I no longer wanted to be part of—especially not that day.

Inside, I saw my old friends again—this time in handcuffs. The patients were being interrogated by the unmasked men. No badges were visible, just authority in its rawest form. It felt less like law enforcement and more like a hostile takeover. We all knew it. I knew it. The workers knew it. The masked men knew it. But these cops were not like the shady Detroit drug crew team—they seemed legit. And this raid seemed legit.

I didn't plan to let them get my wallet. Not this time. Not again. So I performed. Coughing, sneezing, acting sick. I needed to use the bathroom, I claimed. The officer—reluctantly—removed my cuffs. "Hurry up," he mumbled.

There was no cash in my wallet, but my cards were there, and I didn't want to go through the ordeal of canceling everything again. The DMV line had become a recurring nightmare in my life—too many driver's licenses stolen and reissued. So I took my wallet and tucked it into the ceiling tile above the stall, a trick I'd seen in a movie, I think. When I emerged, I was re-frisked and re-cuffed. Business as usual.

Cassie and Amanda were the only two staff working that day. John had called in sick—or maybe he was faking, like me.

From there, we took separate cars to the Warren City Jail. The girls rode in one. I got the solo treatment—my own cruiser. We reunited in the hallway of the booking office. I told them what I always told them in similar situations like this: "Don't say a fucking word. I love you both."

Even in jail, gender dictated geography. I was placed alone in the men's holding cell. Cassie and Amanda were crammed into one with a stoned prostitute. We couldn't talk, but we could see each other through the plexiglassed partitions. We sat there like fish in separate bowls for five hours. The girls passed the time braiding hair. Later, they told me the hooker was "actually kind of cool." I envied their company. Sundays are for church—and in Warren–afternoons, for football and holding tanks.

When we were finally processed out, the cells were just beginning to stir with the post-dinner rush. My wife had arrived too early. If you're ever unfortunate enough to be arrested in Warren, wait until after dinner. That's when the real show begins.

But my evening was far from over.

The fluorescent lights buzzed overhead, casting everything in a flat, sickly yellow. I was leaning on the counter, signing the last of the outprocessing forms, when the door slams open.

In walked Officer Kulhanek—built like a bowling pin, eyes already locked on me. He barely glanced at the desk sergeant.

"I'll handle this guy," he said, low to his partner. Then, to me, "It's you—the piece of shit that was gonna sue me."

It wasn't our first meeting.

We had history. Two years earlier, he had cornered me in the dispensary's parking lot. I barely had one foot out of my car before Kulhanek was in my face. Accusations, questions, slurs—he had a whole routine. His style isn't police work, it's intimidation and douchebaggery. Around the neighborhood and back at the station, they call him "Officer Colonic." You can figure out why.

That day, maybe I asked for his driver's license. Maybe I told him I'd sue if he touched me again. Or maybe I just stood still, calm, while he looked for a reaction he was never going to get. His partner knew the truth: Kulhanek was an asshat in uniform.

At booking he was still the same. Still raving. My name, my mom, my wife—he sprayed it all into the air like bad cologne. I give him nothing.

Kulhanek must not have been a part of the Warren PD "donation" crew—the officers who took monthly envelopes in exchange for letting us breathe a little. Maybe nobody wanted to cut him in. Maybe nobody wanted to stand that close to him. So he freelanced: parking outside the dispensary to scare off patients, pulling them over for nothing, smashing our display cases, initiating raids that went nowhere.

As he was reaching for our patient files during one raid, Amanda had shouted out, "You know that's a HIPAA violation without a warrant, right?"

He froze. Not because he respected the law—because he didn't know it. He had just learned about medical patients' rights from a weed dealer.

Now, in booking, he was trying to drag me back into his tiny penised theater. But I'd learned the only way to win with guys like him is not to buy a ticket.

He returned my shoelaces that were removed during booking. Except... not everything.

"Are my car keys in there?" I asked, gesturing to the plastic bag on the steel table.

That was all it took to set him off.

"Fuck you, you fucking piece of fuckin'..." A tirade of expletives followed, louder and filthier than the last as his saliva landed on my face. Even the hooker from the holding cell was now watching us. Drunks, recently arrested, perked up like nosey neighbors during my home arrests.

It took backup a few more minutes to arrive.

"What the hell is going on in here, Kulhanek?" one officer asked.

After he aired his grievances about me—again—I turned to the "good cop" and asked for my car keys. "It's right here, man," he said, pulling it from the bag and handing it over.

Before I walked out, I caught the eye roll—the universal signal among decent cops that says, "We're not all like him." Then they let me go.

And like that, I was free. Again.

20

Cannabis Goes to the Dogs

I handed the dispensary keys to Jake and walked away from our business—not because they beat me.

Because I finally understood something: they'd burn the whole house down just to keep the roof over their own heads. And I wasn't interested in standing inside that fire anymore—especially with a newborn son. Our firstborn.

But quitting cannabis? Not happening.

I had already been dabbling with hemp years earlier, back before "CBD" was a buzzword. This was still the Wild West of the dispensary era, when most people thought hemp was only good for making rope and hippie sandals.

I bought the URL hempwell.com on a hunch, and started sourcing hemp extract from farms in Kentucky—or at least, that's what the company I purchased it from had represented. Turns out what they resold me was grown in China and packaged in the Bluegrass State.

It doesn't sound great—here's the thing: for a long time, and even today, a huge share of the world's hemp supply chain runs through China. They've used hemp medicinally for thousands of years—long before America was drafting early drafts of the Constitution on hemp paper.

Back then, almost no hemp was being grown domestically in the United States. The law didn't clearly permit it, but it wasn't kicking down doors over it either. It lived in that gray zone—legitimate enough to sell, risky enough to misunderstand, and new enough that everyone in the market was learning in real time.

The oil sold okay. It was marketed and sold as a supplement. I even ended up on a segment with Dr. Sanjay Gupta, which gave Hemp Well a jolt of legitimacy. Back then, you could still pay for CBD ads through Google if you worded things right. But then the pharmaceutical industry came harder than Sheriff Bouchard, Google and Facebook changed their rules, and the fun was over. I shut it down.

Years passed. Then came Ginger's health scare.

A cat that had been handed to us a couple of years earlier by Sarah's grandmother—a woman who never said no to strays. People, animals, didn't matter. If you were in trouble, she'd make you soup, or give you canned cat food and find you a warm bed.

Ginger was tiny, orange and white, and had been abandoned in the Michigan winter at birth. Health problems from day one. By three months, we'd had all her teeth removed. But she was loved.

Four years later, we sat in the vet's office, and the doctor leaned back in her chair with that slow, careful tone vets use when they're really telling you to say goodbye.

"We need to focus on comfort."

We both knew what that meant.

I looked at Sarah. She didn't say a word. I told the vet, "Hold tight."

At home, I went to the back of the cupboard. There it was—one of my old bottles of Chinese CBD oil from an early Hemp Well run. I never told the doctor I was about to give the cat weed. Sarah just watched. What did we have to lose other than Ginger?

One dropper. Then another.

By the next day, Ginger was eating. By the next week, she was moving better. Her eyes had that old brightness again. Sarah looked at me like I'd just pulled off some kind of miracle.

And maybe I had.

That was the moment Hemp Well became more than an idea.

I re-launched it, but this time as a pet wellness brand built on hemp—the quiet cousin of THC. No high. No paranoia. Just relief. And sourced it from inside the United States.

Congress had just legalized hemp-derived products, and I jumped in ahead of the wave. I hired one of the Angels from the dispensary, rented a small warehouse, and started cold-calling.

And if the saying "it's good to have friends" wasn't true, I wouldn't believe any of them.

A friend heard what I was doing and said, "You've got to meet a friend of mine."

Before she became a partner, she'd already built and sold a pet supplement brand to what was, at the time, the biggest player in the pet supplement category. She brought me up to speed fast: sourcing, compliance, formulations, what mattered and what didn't, where people get buried, and where the real opportunities were.

I poured myself into it. A new business, a brand new industry. A legitimate one.

I was reinventing the wheel—again.

I didn't sell "weed" anymore—I helped arthritic Labradors climb stairs again. Our products calmed rescue Chihuahuas who shook through thunderstorms. We gave cats like Ginger not just more time, but more life.

And this time, it stuck.

I did what selling stocks and office buildings had taught me: I pounded the pavement and dialed for dollars.

We grew fast—Petco, Pet Supplies Plus, Amazon, even Target's website and the grocery store my family shopped at for as long as I can remember shopping. Just like the marijuana marketing playbook, no neon crosses or reggae posters. Just clean packaging, an expanded product line, science-backed formulas, and testimonials from pet owners who swore our products saved their animals.

And here's the thing about hemp: it's a gateway drug. Not to harder substances, but to better health.

It gets people reading ingredient labels. Asking questions. Caring more. CBD is one of the first things a lot of people try when they're desperate--like Sarah and I did--and sometimes it works so well that it opens the door to a completely different way of caring for their pets.

Hemp made us pay attention. We started reading the ingredients on every treat and "value" bag of kibble. We avoided cheap fillers. It turned us into better parents to our pets.

Ginger was proof. The vet had given her days. Hemp gave her six more years.

Six years of pawing at the blankets. Six years of curling up next to Sarah at night. Six years of meowing for food at 3 a.m. like she was paying rent.

When she finally left us, it wasn't with that helpless, early ending the vet had written for her. She went on her own terms.

And that's what Hemp Well is really about—giving people and their pets more of the good time.

Of course, success has a scent. And the feds? They never stop sniffing.

I became a target again. Maybe even a bigger one than before. Because when you start winning hearts and minds in places they can't touch—when you chip away at the fear they've spent decades building with something as innocent as a pet treat—they notice.

You want to disrupt the status quo? Show a mom that cannabis can help her golden retriever walk without pain. That's more powerful than any protest sign.

They hated me for that. The NO POT SHOPS crowd expanded their mission.

And I knew it. The war wasn't over—it had just evolved. I wasn't fighting in dispensaries anymore. I was storming the gates of public opinion, one bag of calming chews at a time.

And this time, I had something more powerful than a court ruling or a jury verdict:

A nation of pet owners.

And they don't fuck around when you mess with their pets.

For me, it felt good to be back in business—chasing something I believed was respectable, and safer than selling cannabis.

A picture of Ginger

Inspired by Ginger, Hemp Well has helped support the health and well-being of millions of dogs, cats, birds, and horses.

21

The IRS Audit

In an effort to outrun the raids, the headlines, and the constant harassment, Sarah and I sold our home in Royal Oak and moved north to the lake house we'd built a couple years earlier. The place sat on the same lake that my father had a cabin, the same lake that many of his sisters had little cabins on. And, one of the many places that my Dad lived after retirement. In my head, the lake was simple. Safe. Full of good memories. The kind of place where the noise from the outside world couldn't find you. And at night you could see almost every star in the sky. So when every last aunt, uncle and my dad finally sold their lake cottages, Sarah and I bought a great parcel of land, better than any of them ever had, tore down the existing house and built new.

Sarah took an extended maternity leave. We raised our new son together while I ran Hemp Well remotely, and I tried to convince myself that quiet meant safety.

As the media circus finally dimmed—and the shock of the "N-word video" and the constant raids started to wear off—something else crept in.

Boredom.

The stillness felt less like peace and more like a waiting room. It was boring—too quiet. Maybe I was still shell-shocked and, in some twisted way, missed the grenades being hurled at me. Too much time to think, too much PTSD, too much empty space.

Eventually, we moved back downstate—back to civilization, or whatever passed for it then. We bought a home that fit a growing family and two old cats, in a school district that felt legitimate—one we could actually be proud of.

The chaos, of course, didn't stay behind. Waiting for us wasn't a shady prosecutor or another corrupt cop—it was the IRS.

An audit had been opened—the certified letter informed us, and the mailman. Things were about to get serious. An informal meeting was scheduled.

In the accountant's office My wife and I sat across from Carol in a room with barely enough air conditioning to keep the place cool—an IRS employee who was surprisingly kind and professional, her manner suggesting this might actually be handled like adults. She asked about our income and our businesses—real estate ventures, a media company that managed several websites I owned, and, of course, the dispensaries. We were transparent. We explained the structure: my role; Jake's role; how he was receiving nearly sixty percent of all distributions, a fact our accountants would later confirm in court.

I didn't have much to hide. The problem was I didn't have much to offer, either.

I couldn't explain day-to-day operations. During their meeting, I didn't have QuickBooks access, point-of-sale data, or vendor records. Jake and the cops had those. My lane had always been behind the scenes: damage control, legal strategy, legislative outreach, marketing. I wasn't at the counter. I wasn't moving the product. I was in the background—lobbying Lansing, keeping the legal train on the tracks.

Plus, the cops still hadn't returned a lot of the records—and they didn't plan to.

Between the two hurdles, it was impossible to get through an audit—impossible to answer their questions

Naturally, after that meeting I reached out to Jake for help—he was still running the dispensary we started together and using the same systems we used together.

Crickets.

No call back. No documents. No cooperation. The only paper I could show auditors, aside from my bank records, were years of emails that boiled down to things like, "Jake, how much money did I make this year?" and, from him, "Ryan, you seem stressed—let me buy you out." That was the extent of my knowledge—and my proof.

Because most of the raids landed in 2014, nearly every single personal or business record from that year was seized. Jake still refused to cooperate. My wife and I filed separately and asked the IRS for help locating what the local cops had already taken or what Jake would not share. We got silence.

I even reached out to Jake's accountant, Jim, once Jake went dark. I asked him to pull together anything that could help us reconstruct the year. Jim wasn't just Jake's tax guy; he'd helped us incorporate a few ventures—the food line, some dispensary paperwork, a couple of LLCs. I figured he could at least help with the basics. He sent a few tentative replies, amended one return, and then drifted off. Eventually, he ghosted me too.

The audit dragged on. I brought in more accountants, more lawyers, even a former IRS agent to help sort the mess. Then came a blow that had nothing to do with numbers: Carol—the one person at the IRS who treated this like a fact-finding mission rather than a hunt—got sick. Cancer.

Her file landed on the desk of the IRS's top man in Detroit: John Copenhagen. After I told him how much I liked her, John said she was sick and that he'd be taking over. Then—almost as a footnote—he added that she'd died.

John was no Carol.

From day one, he was aggressive, combative, and convinced of my guilt. "I know it was just you," he told me, flat. After one especially hostile interview, my CPA took me aside and whispered, "This guy's going to be a problem."

He wasn't wrong.

Later I learned John grew up about a half-mile from our Warren dispensary and now lived less than a mile from Jake. A quick look at his public posts showed a pattern of disdain for marijuana—comments like "lazy potheads," and "Watch out, druggies—cops are on the prowl!" aimed at medical-cannabis users.

Reading his thoughts on a screen made me wonder who else John didn't like. Were they sitting in audit rooms like the one I'd sat in? Did he carry the same poison those racist cops did—just in a tie instead of a badge? Was it minorities he resented, women or liberals, or anyone who didn't fit whatever narrow idea of "deserving" he'd built in his head?

Because if his bias showed up that plainly in posts to the public, it had to be leaking into his real job—the quiet, cubicle day job—where he didn't just get to complain about "what's wrong with this country." He got to do something about it. He had a desk, a file, a checklist, and leverage. And the kind of power that looks boring right up until it ruins your life.

Meanwhile, Jake was telling a version that didn't resemble the truth. He met with John, gave multiple interviews, and eventually provided multiple statements to the Department of Justice. In his telling, he was a part time cashier—no management, no banking, no knowledge of finances—despite filing tax returns that listed "Relief Choices Owner" as his occupation. "Ryan ran everything," he said.

"I just worked there part time and ran a logistics consulting company from home." Convenient.

It was obvious to anyone Jake was an owner—that he was lying. But to John, I wasn't just another name on a file. I was the one who brought weed to his town, to his state, and that made me the bigger target. The one worth destroying to satisfy whatever social mission he thought he was on. And once I saw that, it was hard to unsee: John would crucify anyone in that room if he disagreed with them on something he felt strongly about.

Jake wanted nothing to do with the audit. The government wanted nothing to do with Jake. They weren't after him. They were after Al Capone. They were after me.

In prison, the only label worse than CHOMO (child molester) is "rat." If you can't show paperwork proving you're neither, life gets ugly fast. Jake managed to be something worse than a rat—he was a liar. He set me up. And the government granted him the ammunition: full immunity. A license to lie.

It's only perjury if the government says it's perjury.

When the IRS launched its civil audit—the one real chance I had to avoid eventual criminal charges—Jake refused to cooperate. He threw me under the bus without hesitation. Denied his role. Denied access to any remaining documents not stolen by shady cops. Denied knowing anything. Denied, denied, denied—and as the pressure mounted, his story kept shifting.

Right in the middle of that chaos, I later learned—through court filings—that Jake's accountant, Jim, had been sanctioned by the IRS. Two violations tied to Jake's tax return: sloppy work, shady deductions, the kind of amateur-hour accounting that invites audits. He was fined $10,000, warned his license could be yanked, and handed a lifeline: immunity, if he pointed the finger solely at me.

He took it.

Jim knew what he was saying wasn't true—and the government knew it. If you'd met him, you might understand the picture: awkward, jittery, forever in over his head. Total goober is the only way to describe him. He was the kid who probably got shoved into lockers growing up—and probably earned it.

On top of all that, he is a massive pothead—exactly the last person you'd want combing your books or filing with the IRS. Yet there he was, the government's witness, stammering through testimony like he hadn't sat in meetings with both Jake and me for years. As if it were all me. Just me.

His false statements spurred a memory in my hea—a story Jim told me just after the audit started. Years earlier, after his father died and he inherited a commercial building tied to a business that soon collapsed, investigators started asking questions—pointing the finger at Jim over a suspicious fire and the insurance money he received. He said he was pissed off.

Jim may be a goober but as it turns out, a better liar than Jake.

Jake's story to the government about our business partnership would change every time he made official statements. A new and better lie each time.

If he'd simply laid out what he actually did and what I actually did, maybe the narrative would've changed before it calcified.

Just like Doty picked Gary to save, the IRS picked Jake. I was left holding the bag.

They didn't care that Jake received the majority of the income. They didn't care that I had no access to books or sales data. They cared about a conviction. I was their Capone. Because, like Al Capone, I had beaten all the state charges. And like Capone, they decided taxes would be the hammer.

That's when I learned the hell that is IRS Code §280E. The modern equivalent of asset forfeiture for legal dispensaries.

Under 280E, anyone engaged in the sale of a Schedule I substance—like cannabis—is forbidden from deducting any business expenses from their federal taxes. Not payroll. Not rent. Not copy paper for the printer. Not even the money paid to employees. That meant Jake's 58% payout as a part time 'employee'—fully taxed and reported—was still counted as my income. And none of it was considered a legitimate business deduction.

Even the money extorted (stolen) by dirty cops like Eric Smith, Lt. Hansberry, Doty and Sheriff Bouchard? Not deductible. Legal fees to Neil? Not deductible.

Even though that obscure code had been sitting on the books since the 1980s—written to deter crack cocaine dealers—it didn't really get dusted off and used in earnest until after I'd already exited the industry, when thousands of dispensaries were popping up across America.

Dispensaries across the country are still grappling with this broken system.

Seven days before the statute of limitations expired—I was indicted.

Charged with tax evasion. The only person in American history criminally charged, convicted and then sent to jail by applying the unconstitutional but legitimate 280E tax code as their basis.

I was also charged with one count of lying to a government official—for telling Agent Copenhagen that Jake was my business partner and that I was not involved in the day-to-day operations.

By this point, I hated Jake. Hated his fat frame. Every good memory had flipped on me, and I started replaying the past like it had always been loaded—like the warning signs were there the whole time and I just refused to see them.

Time—and a little gunpowder—has a way of doing that: rewriting history, and rewriting your memories.

Before Nixon declared war on marijuana, the federal government had already made lawful possession nearly impossible: unless you had a marijuana tax stamp, you were a criminal.

22

The Lawyers

When you become the face of a fledgling industry—particularly one as misunderstood, reviled, and hastily legislated as medical marijuana—you don't just attract pioneers and idealists. You attract opportunists. Parasites. Crusaders. And above all: lawyers.

I could fill volumes with their names and invoices. In truth, Jake and I spent more time around attorneys than we ever did with growers. Which says everything you need to know about how cannabis entered the mainstream—not through soil and grow lights, but through subpoenas and the smoke of courtroom theatrics.

The first attorney I hired was Neil Rockind in 2010.

If you squinted, Neil could've passed for a Hollywood prosecutor. Handsome. Smooth. Dangerous in a courtroom. He had made his name in Oakland County, best known for orchestrating the conviction of Jack Kevorkian—"Dr. Death," the man who dared to offer the terminally ill a dignified exit.

Had I done my research, I might've run the other way. Kevorkian was a hero in my house. My grandmother, wasting away in a nursing home during those same years, would have chosen his path if it were legal. Our family didn't see Dr. Death as a monster. We saw him as mercy. But Neil had come recommended. And to his credit, he never brought Kevorkian up. Neither did I.

Instead, Neil became a paradox: a man who'd once thrown people in cages for challenging orthodoxy, now defending those doing the

135

same. He transitioned from prosecutor to protector. From the dark side to the green rush. And he was damn good at it.

Neil had no illusions about morality. He played to win. Putting Jack Kevorkian behind bars or getting Ryan Richmond out of them—it made no difference. It was the scoreboard that mattered. And in this world, morality was a liability.

Eventually, I came to see that prosecutors weren't much different. County. State. Federal. They weren't in pursuit of truth. They were in pursuit of numbers. A win was a win—even if it meant bending the law until it cracked. Even if it meant aiming rifles at patients and pregnant women, ignoring facts and putting innocent people in cages.

If Neil was a "Rockweiler"—a predator you kept on a leash until blood needed spilling—then Paul was something else entirely.

Paul had wandered into law after his punk rock band crashed and burned. He didn't litigate—he loitered. Ran background checks. Smoothed things over after minor raids. Provided representation for employees caught up in raids. Negotiated plea deals for growers caught up in the harassment. Sometimes he got paid in weed. Sometimes he smoked his retainer. What was left, he passed to Jake, who turned it into cash and sold it at the dispensaries.

Paul wasn't dangerous. He was just... present. He wanted more than billables. He wanted in. He pushed for equity, partnerships, advisory roles. Jake and I opened a dispensary and doctor clinic with Paul. Ran an advocacy non-profit together, the Marijuana Patients Organization. But when the raids came and I needed support, Paul melted into the woodwork, suddenly "just a lawyer" unwilling to testify on our behalf or disclose his involvement.

Despite it all, I liked Paul and considered him a friend. He had no delusions. No killer instinct. But he showed up—sometimes high, sometimes unshaven, and sometimes very useful.

Then there were the ghosts. The appellate lawyers. The ones behind the scenes, writing motions in legal basements or from spare bedrooms. They didn't wear nice suits. They wore exhaustion. But they were smart—smarter than Paul, smarter than Neil, and smarter than the judges.

Eventually, I found myself relying on them the most. Because Michigan had legalized medical marijuana, but the people tasked with enforcing the law were openly hostile to it. Votes didn't matter when revenue was on the line. Pot funded the system: court fees, forfeitures, pensions. I wasn't a criminal. I was competition.

Attorney General Bill Schuette. County Prosecutors Jessica Cooper and Eric Smith. The No Pot Shops legal department. They weren't enforcing the law. They were protecting a pipeline. When they realized marijuana was the Trojan Horse—an open door toward full-scale legalization—they reacted like all regimes do when threatened: they struck first.

And when that wasn't enough, the feds followed. If the city, county, or state couldn't take you down, they had one last option: call in the cavalry.

Enter Robert Vanwert—one of the federal prosecutors on my eventual federal criminal case, his name affixed to the filings like a stamp. And then there were the rumors: ties to the shadow government, "see-eye-ehhhhh"—the kind of connection you don't confirm, you just learn to factor in.. His case list included organized deadly crime syndicates, murderous drug dealing biker gangs, January 6 leaders, and, bizarrely, me and my "boring' IRS case. Assigned to the DOJ's Violent and Organized Crime Unit, Vanwert wasn't laughing off my advocacy. He was targeting it.

I didn't hear about any of this from a newspaper or a podcast. I would eventually learn it walking the track in federal prison. My friend Shane—another inmate—had been on the other side of the badge. He told me what most people never hear out loud: every drug unit in America, like Doty's crew, has a federal hand in it and a Van Wert as the operative. Usually it's always CIA-linked, even if it doesn't say "CIA" on the paycheck. Just like forward military units always have an intelligence officer embedded, domestic narcotics teams have their own "liaison."

Since the Patriot Act, he said, the government didn't just loosen the leash—it cut it off. Warrantless searches on Americans, mass wiretaps, dragnet surveillance. His job had been to mine the data, listen to phone calls, figure out who was moving drugs, then whisper tips to local, county, or state law enforcement. "Blue van on I-75 at 4:30," he'd say. They'd make the routine traffic stop for a lane change violation. They didn't know Shane's title or his agency. They didn't need to. They always listened. And why wouldn't they? They got to keep 70% of whatever they seized. The ones too "American" — too righteous — to go along with it got cut off from federal funding until they fell in line.

He told me that he hadn't voted for Obama but at least respected the attempt to build a national police department instead of running on illegal spying and kickbacks. He tried to stay in the game long enough to clean up his own community's meth and heroin problem, but when he busted the wrong people—guys on the county sheriff's kickback team—the hammer came down. They framed him, the feds swooped in, he was open and honest with them, and he ended up walking the same prison yard with me.

"If I had just shut my mouth," he'd say. "I knew the world I lived in."

Get with the program or go to jail. Cop or medical-marijuana dispensary owner—it didn't matter. Legitimacy is decided by the deciders.

Out on that track, he helped me connect the dots. He reviewed my filings, walked me through my statements, and used two decades of intelligence work to decode the names and roles in my case. It confirmed what lawyers had been telling me for years: there was a bigger element at play here. That's how I began to see the architecture of the machine that had crushed me.

And the irony was thick. The DEA and the U.S. government still insists marijuana is more dangerous than alcohol—even fentanyl.

I'd known hundreds of people who used marijuana throughout my life. I'd only known two who used fentanyl—two I knew well. Both were dead before forty.

* * *

When my federal indictment arrived next-day air as opposed to SWAT teams and tanks, I needed a different kind of attorney. Not a pot shop litigator. A soldier. I was a veteran—I knew the federal government played for keeps.

I Googled names. Read bios. Checked records. I had never met anyone who'd gone to a federal trial. I didn't know what qualified someone as a good federal lawyer. But I knew I needed one. Fast.

Michael Bullotta stood out. A retired U.S. assistant attorney specializing in governmental corruption. Credited with sending Detroit's disgraced mayor, Kwame Kilpatrick, to prison. More importantly, he had put away Eric Smith—the Macomb County prosecutor responsible for raiding our dispensaries and stealing hundreds of thousands of my family's dollars. If anyone could understand my case, it would be Bullotta.

I emailed him that night. He called the next morning. Two days later we met in his Detroit office—shabby, but close to the courthouse.

He told me about Kilpatrick. Tried to impress me. I waved it off. "I could have convicted Kwame," I said. What I wanted to hear about was tax evasion. Government corruption. Eric Smith.

Bullotta shared stories I hadn't heard. He told me most political corruption involved tax fraud—nobody wants to report illegal kickbacks. Politicians charged with corruption routinely faced additional tax evasion charges. He knew the IRS prosecutor on my case: Mark MacDonald.

"Everyone calls him Mack," Bullotta said. "Except behind his back at the US Attorney's office. We call him 'The Robot.'"

"Is that because he's a machine in court?" I asked.

"No," Bullotta replied. "Because he's a weird fucking dude."

That part, I didn't doubt.

We settled on a fee. I handed over the check. Made it clear—again—that I intended to go to trial. Take the stand. Tell the truth. No plea deals. He nodded. Filed his appearance. And then... silence.

A year passed with the weight of trial hanging over my head. Unlike my earlier cases, I didn't play lawyer at night. I didn't get online trying to learn what attorneys pick up their first year of law school. Fifteen years of fighting—coupled with two young kids—sat heavy on me. This time, I put my faith fully in Bullotta.

Just short of two months before trial, Bullotta called me into his office and told me: "I have a new practice, a new family. Your case is too political. I can't move forward."

No refund. Just a polite exit and a letter to the judge suggesting I was the problem—an "irreconcilable breakdown in communication." Like we were filing for divorce.

Something felt off about him calling me into the office that day, so before I even walked in I turned on the voice recorder on my phone. Later, when I told him the conversation was recorded, he didn't get angry. He got cold.

"I still have friends at the DOJ," he said. "I'd watch what you do. Carefully."

I never told the court what he said. I was scared.

The government—and the court—treated the whole thing like a divorce I'd engineered. Like I was delaying the trial. Like Bullotta withdrawing as my counselor was all my fault.

I wasn't stalling. I was flailing.

The judge gave me two weeks to find new counsel. The trial date was already on the calendar for later that month.

I certainly wasn't going to the internet to find another Bullotta, so I asked around my limited sphere—lawyers who knew state cases, friends from the poker league who did personal injury, a few my cousin knows a guy names—but nobody I trusted really knew the federal world.

A few old headline cases came up—big, splashy things that made the papers many years earlier—and through all the noise, one name kept resurfacing.

One name stood out. Enter Deday Larene.

His name sounded like a Marvel villain, but the story checked out: born on D-Day, 1944. I needed a fighter. What I got was a fossil.

Deday had once defended mobsters. Literal bloodlines from Al Capone's empire. His big win? Arguing that the blood in a suspect's trunk wasn't from Jimmy Hoffa—it was fish blood. Only in America.

Weeks later, after I handed over a $100,000 check, I learned Deday had done six months in Morgantown Federal Prison—charged with extortion and tax evasion. Sentenced to the same prison I would eventually call home.

His partner, Mark—only slightly younger and way more creepy than the octogenarian—told me, "Who better to represent you than someone who's gone to jail for tax evasion?"

Our meetings were brief. They never filed a single motion or offered a single objection. Never called a witness. Promised expert witnesses–former IRS agents that never materialized. They weren't ready for the short deadline to trial start date. Not for federal prosecutors. Not for the IRS. Not for VanWert and the CIA. Not for Mack "The Robot."

Well—I take that back. They did file one objection: "We're not ready. We need more time." The judge denied their motion.

My appellate lawyer would later write it plainly in describing Deday and Mark: "Completely ineffective."

Looking back, I might've been better off with Paul. At least he worked for weed.

23

The Trial

By the time the trial rolled around, I'd been in plenty of rooms with lawyers. Defense tables littered with Styrofoam coffee cups. Pre-trial conferences where attorneys spoke in a kind of coded language—legal shorthand mixed with personal history. The back corner of some rented office space where we'd prep for a hearing while trying to ignore the constant cell phone interruption.

But this was different.

This wasn't a conference table. This was the stage. The big one. The day where I'd be front and center in a real courtroom, with real stenographers and jury foremen, where every cough, every shuffled paper, every poorly timed whisper became part of the permanent record.

My first case in Ferndale—Clinical Relief—ended in a dismissal a few years earlier, because by then marijuana was legal for both the sick and the healthy. Seven long years after it began.

The twenty other raids that ended in actual charges being filed? All bark, no bite. All of them died during pre-trial conferences. The system blinked. The clock ran out. The prosecutions collapsed under their own weight.

But this was a federal case? This one was different.

TV teaches you to expect a certain majesty—sweeping shots of the judge's bench, speeches that end in applause, a swelling soundtrack. Justice in slow motion. But the reality is that the prosecutor walks past you in the hallway like you're just another coworker, like you're there to discuss quarterly planning concerns instead of whether you'll spend the next decade in a cage.

You want him to trip. Spill coffee down his shirt. Maybe get clipped by a truck outside. He wants you to disappear.

A lawyer friend once summed up federal court for me: "It's the place where everyone's polite, everyone's professional, and everyone gets twenty years."

If I'd had a choice, I'd have rather come in through the back door, shackled and chained. At least that would have been honest. It would have been less awkward than pretending we were all here for some polite, mutually agreed-upon exercise in fairness.

After the jury was selected from a pool of people I wouldn't consider peers in this lifetime or the next—folks not brave enough to get out of jury duty, or too bored to stay home—the next day the United States Government rolled in carts stacked with files and papers. Thick banker's boxes, heavy enough to make the wheels squeal, full of what they wanted the jury to think was evidence.

I knew most of it would never be opened. Never be touched. Never actually connect to anything I'd done. It was volume as intimidation—empty weight dressed up like truth.

They weren't just bringing exhibits. They were setting the mood.

Props for the performance. A visual meant to whisper to the jury before anyone spoke: look how much he did. Look how guilty he must be.

My lawyers walked in carrying two manila folders. And even that, they managed to stumble through.

This wasn't a trial. It was theater.

And the feds had the bigger stage crew.

If it had been a wedding, their side of the aisle was overflowing. Law students from the nearby law college in pressed suits. Courthouse clerks popping in during their breaks. IRS agents from the Detroit field offices lined up in the benches like they were front row at a prizefight. Even a couple of the NO POT SHOPS crew, there to watch the curtain call on a story they'd been helping write for years.

I felt completely alone—like I was standing on an auction block, while everyone in the room circled and sized me up, waiting their turn to bid.

But I did have one thing on my side? Sarah. Always Sarah. And one weird juror who had been dismissed earlier in the week but came back to watch. He said he thought I was innocent before he'd even heard the opening statements. Maybe he was telling the truth. Maybe he was just bored. Maybe he had already told work he was out for jury duty and just wanted to see how a real trial went down, because God knows it wasn't going to look anything like it does on TV.

The government started rolling out their witnesses like an assembly line.

First, the IRS agents and then my old nemesis Copenhagen from the audit. They didn't just testify; they lectured. They walked the jury through 26 U.S.C. § 280E like they were teaching a tax seminar to seasoned accountants, skipping over the inconvenient truth: that this statute is enforced almost exclusively against marijuana businesses because they are licensed. Not heroin dealers. Not coke traffickers. Not the black-market fentanyl kings killing friends of mine. Just marijuana. Literally just me.

My lawyers opened by going after Copenhagen—defending me against the charge that I'd lied to a government official: him.

Lawyer: Here, of course, in this courtroom, these kinds of mistakes don't pass unnoticed, because we have a court reporter who writes everything down—or records it—so that if there's ever a misunderstanding between us about Pontiac, Detroit, or anything else, we can go back and review the court reporter's record, right?

John: Sure.

Lawyer: Now, you could have done that. In any of your interviews, you could have had a court reporter—or some other recorder—during any interview with Mr. Richmond, isn't that right?

John: No. We do not do that.

Lawyer: Okay. But you could have. You could have.

John: Only—rarely. The only time we do any type of recording is if the taxpayer is recording as well, and then we will record on our end.

What John didn't say on the stand was the simplest part: I didn't have money. It was gone—taken in the raids. And Jake wasn't some innocent bystander. He was my partner, the one who ran off with whatever cash still existed, and whatever paperwork and insight an audit would've needed to resolve things civilly. I told John that—plainly.

If John recorded anything at all, it may not even be audible—not through the bad-cop routine he got to play out, all the yelling during our sit-downs meant to drown out the truth. In the witness box, he was quiet and polite.

The paper trail didn't match the story they were selling the jury, and they knew it. But omissions make great props—so they cut those pages from the script and hoped no one noticed.

They knew my lawyers wouldn't object. It was half past nap time.

Then came the rep—flown in on the government's dime from Austin—representing the point-of-sale system Jake had set up, customized, and used. My name was on the account with Jake's, sure, but I'd barely touched it.

He testified like he'd been in the shop every day, watching me ring up customers, when in reality all he'd ever seen was my name on an old file. He didn't even work for the company when we used the system. And the company that originally provided the software had different ownership back then—eventually acquired by his—so he was testifying about a product and a time he wasn't actually part of.

And then came Ryan's Angels.

The feds must have thought they'd hit the jackpot. They paid their travel and meal expenses, brought them in like they were star witnesses who'd break me apart with some insider bombshell. Instead, they told the truth. And the truth was simple: Jake was Ryan's partner. Ryan was not involved day-to-day. Period. End of story.

They painted the same picture I'd tried to explain to John and the IRS—one that didn't match the government's story at all.

On the stand, under oath, Amanda described me as an occasional visitor, not a daily operator. A ghost, more than a presence behind the counter. Jake, she said, was the constant—handling the money, running the place, working with the managers, doing the day-to-day that actually makes a dispensary function. And the truth was, that's exactly how Jake and I structured it.

Then the transcript turned that reality into clean, brutal black-and-white:

Lawyer: You said that it was your understanding that Jacob Schell and Ryan Richmond owned Relief Choices; is that correct?

Amanda: Yes.

Lawyer: And it was Jacob Schell who handled the finances, correct?

Amanda: As far as I know, yeah.

Lawyer: And never once did you deliver cash to Mr. Richmond, correct?

Amanda: No.

Lawyer: And when Mr. Richmond would come in once or twice a week, if that, it would be just for a few minutes at a time, correct?

Amanda: Yes.

That's not a misunderstanding. That's a structure.

And when the subject turned to raids, Amanda didn't speak in theories—she spoke in inventory and damage, and in the three times she'd been handcuffed for doing her job. The kind of details you remember because you're the one left standing in the wreckage afterward, sweeping up glass and trying to make the place look neat again.

Lawyer: And you said there were three raids you were involved.

Amanda: Yes.

Lawyer: And in each of these raids, product was taken, cash was taken, equipment was taken, supplies were taken, correct?

Amanda: The last two times. The very first time they only took the weed and cash.

Lawyer: And was there damage done that had to be repaired?

Amanda: I mean, yeah. They were pretty rough with stuff and would break stuff and leave it a mess.

Then the prosecutor—cold, mechanical, the Robot—tried to reframe it as orderly law enforcement. "Execution of a search warrant." Like it was paperwork, not a shakedown.

U.S. Attorney: ...that's what it was, right, the execution of a search warrant?

Amanda: I mean—

U.S. Attorney: Or you don't know?

Amanda: We asked them for a search warrant and—

U.S. Attorney: You asked them for a search warrant? You, personally?

Amanda: I probably did, yes... they probably told me they don't need one, so—

Amanda probably did ask for a warrant. Most of the time it wasn't "law enforcement" in any meaningful sense—it was armed thugs in blue, there to take what they could take. She only spoke about the bloodier raids, the ones that stayed with you.

And her answer cracked the varnish.

Because she wasn't describing some neat, lawful procedure. She was describing force. Intimidation. Theft wearing a uniform.

At one point she mentioned being "robbed" by Detroit police officers—Hansberry and Watson—names that didn't need explaining in that courtroom. The judge knew exactly who they were. She'd sentenced them a few years earlier. Amanda wasn't speculating. She was pointing at a pattern the government either ignored—or never bothered to understand. It's too bad the jury never got educated enough by my lawyers to see what she was really saying.

Cassie's testimony was nearly identical. Same ownership understanding. Same division of labor. Same reality: Jake handled the cash, the finances, the day-to-day. Two witnesses, separate lives, telling the same story.

The prosecutor could feel it slipping, because you could see his jaw tighten as the answers landed. It wasn't going the way they'd planned.

What they were saying directly contradicted Jake's version—the version the government wanted. And that was the sick part: these women were handing the court the missing piece in plain language. Jake was my partner. Jake ran the shop. Jake handled the money. Information he never offered. Information I never had, because I wasn't the one doing it.

Four versions of the same truth would've been stronger than two. But they didn't want strength. They wanted a story that fit their charge sheet.

So they limited the witnesses—chose not to call the other two employees—tightened their grip on the narrative and tried to keep the truth from multiplying in front of the jury. Because once the same story comes from enough mouths, you can't unhear it.

I was told later by Amanda that as they waited in the witness room, the Angels didn't exactly keep their thoughts to themselves. The room was cramped, government lights buzzing overhead. The Angels — were waiting, arms crossed, energy sharp as glass.

Jake sat on a chair too small for his wide frame in the corner of the cramped witness holding room, avoiding their eyes, pretending to read the floor tiles.

Amanda and Cassie couldn't stand the sight of him—even though Cassie had married his first cousin. Being in the same room with him felt wrong, like the air changed the second he walked in. The tension was so thick Amanda told me later they all asked the court administrator, politely, "Is it okay if we sit in the hallway?" The hallway didn't even have chairs.

Trinity was the only one who didn't bother pretending. She made comments under her breath, loud enough for people to catch, because she wasn't interested in sparing anyone's comfort. They all knew what was coming. They all knew he'd lied before—to investigators, to anyone willing to write it down and call it a statement.

And now he was about to do it again in open court.

Trinity looked at him and asked, "Are you going to tell the truth today?"

Jake shifted in his chair, pretending not to hear.

Then Jake left the witness room and was escorted into the courtroom. The heavy double doors swung open.

I hadn't seen him—hadn't spoken to him—in a decade.

He shuffled in and took the slow walk to the witness stand, guided like a man being delivered. The gallery went silent. The tension settled over the room, thick enough to taste.

Sarah sat behind me, both of us staring hard.

The bailiff stepped forward and asked Jake to do something he hadn't done in a decade.

"Raise your right hand. Do you swear to tell the truth, the whole truth, and nothing but the truth?"

Jake raised his hand. His voice trembled, just slightly.

"I do."

He sat. Papers shuffled. The Robot stepped forward with the first question. But I wasn't listening to the words. I was locked in on Jake.

Sarah and I both wanted to unload on him. But we didn't. We just stared.

Sarah gripped the wooden bench, knuckles white. Jake kept his eyes fixed on the prosecutor, the carpet, anywhere but our way. If looks could talk, mine would've been censored before the first sentence finished. Sarah's glare wasn't much softer.

Jake shifted again, his shoulders sagging under the invisible weight of our stares. His eyes flicker, almost — almost — in our direction, then snap back to the carpet in front of him.

He never looked at us. Not once. Not at me. Not at Sarah. But he felt it. You could see it in the way his body bent, like silence weighed more than any question that the prosecutor could ask. I hoped he would tell the truth, come clean, help me out.

The courtroom was silent except for Jake's shaky answers — and the mountain of his lies filling the room.

His story had evolved over the years—one version for the IRS, another for the DOJ, and now a new one that had changed again earlier that week. The government handed this latest version to my lawyers right before trial, and now he was about to deliver it to a jury like it had always been true.

His newest version? That he wanted to be my business partner.

U.S. Attorney: Were you an owner of Relief Choices?

Jake: I was not.

U.S. Attorney: Did you want to be an owner of Relief Choices?

Jake: I did.

U.S. Attorney: Did you discuss that with Mr. Richmond?

Jake: We did.

U.S. Attorney: Okay. And what was his response to you wanting to be an owner?

Jake: He thought it would be a better idea if we set up different businesses and had a business-to-business relationship.

U.S. Attorney: Okay. Did he explain why he thought that would be a better idea?

Jake: He did.

U.S. Attorney: And what was his reason?

Jake: If we got raided or if something bad happened, then he could take control of it and control the situation better and I would be protected.

U.S. Attorney: Okay. And you said you weren't an owner of Relief Choices. Who was the owner of Relief Choices?

Jake: Ryan Richmond.

U.S. Attorney: And to the best of your knowledge, did Mr. Richmond have any partners in Relief Choices?

Jake: I do not believe so.

"I do not believe so."

What the hell, I thought. He knew every single detail—every trade secret, every interaction, every little behind-the-counter rhythm. This was a man pretending not to know too much, the same man who used to brag to anyone who would listen—I'm the boss—especially the strippers at the clubs he frequented. He wanted the world to know he owned a dispensary—a business.

A little performance to cover old insecurities, the residue of being a fat kid and then a dead-end job seeker after college. And now, under oath, suddenly he wasn't sure who else—besides me—was the boss.

When questioned by my attorney, he tried to draw a clean line between the two dispensaries—admitting partnership once, then denying it everywhere else it mattered. Relief Choices was on trial that day, not Clinical Relief.

> Lawyer: Okay. But it's your testimony that even though you had been an owner or partner in Clinical Relief [with the Colorado crew], you were not a partner or owner to any extent in Relief Choices; that's your testimony?
>
> Jake: Yes.

Then the defense walked him back to January 26, 2012 to Relief Choices in Warren—when two Warren officers, Johnson and Pylack, came by.

> Lawyer: ...you were visited by a couple of Warren police officers named Johnson and Pylak... Do you remember that?
>
> Jake: Yes.
>
> Lawyer: ...they wanted to look around... You were nice enough to let them in... right?
>
> Jake: Yes.
>
> Lawyer: And you told them that you are a co-owner of the business commonly referred to as Relief Choices. Do you recall that, sir?
>
> Jake: I do not recall that.

The most common response Jake gave that day was "I do not recall"—unless the question was slow pitched by the government and helped pin everything on me.

"I do not recall" is the safest sentence in a witness's toolbox, and it's what the government lawyers coached Jake to say that day. In court, perjury isn't about being wrong—it's about knowingly saying something false about a material fact. If a witness answers, "I don't recall," it's far harder to prove intent, because memory is slippery and private. You can't cross-examine a blank space the way you can cross-examine a lie.

Then my lawyer handed Jake the police report—the one where he'd identified himself as a co-owner—just to help him "recall."

> Lawyer: ...you did tell the Officers Johnson and Pylak that you were a co-owner... right?
>
> Jake: It looks like that's what they wrote down, but I don't recall that.

If you've been following along, you'll remember Officer Johnson—the one who later got sued and wound up personally on the hook for part of the damages after he referred to his coworker DeSheila Howlett as his "slave girl" and the "Gorilla Glue gorilla."

Officer Pylak had his own mess, too: he eventually was charged with a misdemeanor for obtaining money under false pretenses. The ending—like so many endings in this story—didn't feel like accountability so much as paperwork: a back door deal, a resignation, and $20,000 paid back to the City of Warren.

My lawyer then walked the timeline forward to the next visit—July 12, 2012—this time Sergeant Okray.

Lawyer: ...you received another visit... Sergeant Okray. Do you remember that?

Jake: Yes.

Lawyer: ...they wanted to come in and you let them into the Relief Choices, correct?

Judge: Do you recall doing that?

Jake: I don't recall letting them in.

Lawyer: Do you recall... you told Sergeant Okray that you were currently the co-owner of Relief Choices?

Jake: I don't recall that conversation.

My lawyer handed him another signed police report and said "read it at your leisure"—then asked again.

Lawyer: ...do you now recall that you told Sergeant Okray that you were a co-owner of Relief Choices?

Jake: I don't recall that conversation.

Sergeant Okray is another man with a past of his own. Years earlier, after Law Enforcement Night at a Detroit Tigers game at Comerica Park, he was arraigned on two misdemeanors—disorderly person (intoxicated) and possession of a weapon while under the influence—after a fight with a Detroit police officer in 2015. The charges were dropped. A couple years after that, he was promoted to lieutenant.

In Warren, Michigan, that's how the prizes get handed out: not for restraint, not for judgment—just for staying inside the lines of the right side of 8 Mile.

Then came the paper that didn't rely on memory: the signature card and paperwork to open the business bank account.

> Lawyer: ...this is a signature card for Relief Choices...
> and it identifies you... a member... just like it identifies Mr.
> Richmond. A member is an owner of a limited liability cor-
> poration, isn't it?
> Jake: I suppose it could be.
> Lawyer: You suppose it could be anything else?
> Jake: I—

And then the tax return—his own handwriting in the language of
the IRS.

> Lawyer: You filed an income tax return, didn't you...?
> Jake: Yes.
> Lawyer: ...the business name... on Schedule C... was Re-
> lief Choices, wasn't it?
> Jake: That's what it says.
> Lawyer: It is what it says.

This is where the government's theory started to wobble. Because
you don't "accidentally" put a business on your Schedule C. You don't
"accidentally" become a member on the signature card. Those aren't
accidents. Those are choices.

And then they got to the part that made Jake's denial feel absurd:
the money—and the tax figures.

Jake: A lot of credit card services didn't like doing business with medical marijuana, and if they found out you were doing medical marijuana transactions with credit cards, they would shut the service down.

U.S. Attorney: Okay. When they stopped accepting credit card payments for Relief Choices, what did the company do— meaning Relief Choices?

Jake: We opened up a credit card service through Schell Group.

That one answer did more than he realized. He said we, but the "we" eventually ran straight through his company—Schell Group—because that's where the processing lived. Not in Relief Choices' name. Not in mine. In his. His business. His control.

But details like that didn't matter to the government. Not the kind of details that point in the wrong direction.

Lawyer: ...one of the things you did was you would tell Mr. Richmond how much money he had received as a payout from the operation.

Jake: I don't understand your question.

Lawyer: Do you recall... an email... telling him how much you received from the business that year?

Jake: I don't recall.

Lawyer: ...a spreadsheet showing the payments received from... Relief Choices?

Jake: I sent him many spreadsheets, specifically I don't recall.

Jake was then handed a printed copy of an email exchange between us—the kind we'd traded every year, back when we were still operating like partners.

Subject line: tax time.
"Jake how much money did I make this year?"

Then the lawyer widened the frame—motive, resentment, the breakup.

Lawyer: There came a time when you and Mr. Richmond just weren't getting along, correct?
Jake: Yes.
Lawyer: ...around 2014?
Jake: Yeah... Sounds about right.
Lawyer: And you haven't spoken to Mr. Richmond since.
Jake: No.
Lawyer: ...Mr. Richmond... calls it quits... I'm getting out... right?
Jake: Yes.
Lawyer: You, however, continued, correct?
Jake: Yes.

On redirect, the prosecutor tried to mop up the contradictions with a shrug.

U.S. Attorney: Why did you report Relief Choices on your Schedule C?

Jake: I don't know.

U.S. Attorney: Were you the owner of Relief Choices that year?

Jake: No.

And then—"no more questions, "your honor". Like the government didn't want the jury sitting too long with the obvious.

Finally, the defense said the quiet part out loud: Jake didn't just have a story—he had an audience.

Lawyer: ...No one at this table ever told you to do anything other than tell the truth, right?

Jake: Yes, sir.

Lawyer: Okay. But you know what they wanted to hear, didn't you? ...that Ryan Richmond was the sole and only owner...

Jake: Yes.

And then the line that hung in the air because it was the only line that explained everything—why his memory failed so precisely, why his story kept evolving, why the truth always stopped just short of implicating him.

Lawyer: ...by keeping your answers consistent with what the Government wanted to hear... you knew... you would never have to sit in that chair [my chair]. You might have to cut a check, but beats sitting in that chair, doesn't it?

Jake: I never thought about it like that.

Lawyer: Didn't think about keeping your freedom by telling the Government what you knew they wanted to hear?

Jake: Nope.

Lawyer: Nope.

And there it was: a man insisting he wasn't an owner, wasn't a partner, didn't recall the conversations where he called himself one—while his signature card, his Schedule C, and his tax-time spreadsheets told a different story.

Not guilty of ownership—guilty of convenience. "I was paid well. I didn't ask questions."

Bank records proved he got paid more than me, if anyone was counting. And while my lawyers could have hammered harder at him on the stand, not stumbled throughout the trial, had filed a single motion, the truth was my fate had already started sliding the last time Jake even spoke to me. That was right when the IRS audit began sniffing around — the moment the noose first tightened.

If Jake had come clean then, if he had stood up and told the truth — not some complete fabrication or half-story, not the evolving fiction he fed them — maybe things would have turned out different. He held information no one else had. He was in the books, in the day-to-day, in the conversations with accountants and vendors and staff. He had the keys to unlock the whole picture. And if he had laid it out back then, maybe both of us would have been sitting in a different room that day, on the outside instead of under the fluorescent lights of a cold and sterile courtroom.

But that's not what he did. He kept his mouth shut when it mattered, and opened it only when it served him. By the time he finally decided to talk, the narrative was already written — I was the target, the villain, the headline, Al Capone. His silence in those early days wasn't just absence. It was an act all its own.

Knowing his deceit was slowly being revealed, he saved his best lie for last.

It wasn't in discovery. This was brand new—and it mattered. The government is required to warn you about testimony like this, but they hadn't. They were hearing it for the first time, the same as me and the lawyers. Jake knew his agreement with the government.

Unprovoked—and not asked by either side, not mine and not the government's—he looked at the jury and said:

"One day Ryan came to the dispensary, grabbed $25,000 in cash, and said it was for the IRS."

Flat. Out. Lie.

We never kept that kind of cash in the stores. Ever. The money left every single day, usually to Jake's own home safe, just like the Angels testified to. From there, it went to pay growers or suppliers. He was the one handling it, not me. Even before trial, I'd trusted him not to have sticky fingers. Looking back, I'm not sure why.

With a raid every twenty-six days on average, it would have been insane to keep that much cash sitting around. That supposed "IRS payment" he was talking about? It would have represented an entire week's worth of cash revenue. It never happened.

But Jake and my lawyers both knew what his immunity deal required: put me in a cage.

The years of income I'd helped supply his family, the laughs we'd shared, the self-employed lifestyle he'd been able to enjoy, the title of 'boss' he wore proudly because we'd built something together—none of it meant anything now. Maybe his biggest motivator was what happened two years into the audit and five years earlier: his wife passed away, leaving him alone with three kids. I can't imagine that pain. If I'm being honest, the stress might have broken me, too.

Driving home from court that day, Sarah said, "If you were dead and I had the kids alone, I would say anything I needed to."

She wasn't wrong. I couldn't imagine losing Sarah.

Jake and I—we weren't the better half in either of our marriages. We weren't the glue. We weren't the muscle. We weren't the rock that kept everything from coming apart. We were the ones who got held together.

But Jake's lie didn't start after Becky died. It started long before that. When the audit first started, when he told his first lie.

And that part—I couldn't forgive.

When my turn in the hot seat finally came, my lawyer opened with softballs — questions meant to humanize me in front of the jury.

> Lawyer: Do you have children?
> Me: I do.

My voice started to crack.

> Lawyer: What are their ages and names and genders?
> This is one of the easier ones.
> Me: Six and eight.

I saw my son looking up at me, asking if I wanted to shoot hoops on the little indoor mini basketball set, and my daughter climbing onto my back for another piggyback ride. Their faces were so innocent it hurt to look at them in my mind.

Halfway through saying "six" and "eight" out loud, I broke. Full sob. Couldn't stop it. Sarah was crying. The stenographer was crying. I saw two jurors wipe their eyes.

It wasn't a performance. It was raw. It was the most intense, unfiltered moment of my life — more than any raid, more than sentencing, more than the times I'd thought I might actually die at the hands of law enforcement. Or when I lost my mother.

> Lawyer: Okay. Would you like some water, sir?
> Me: Zach and Sloane.
> Lawyer: Zachary, I take it, is a boy, and he's the eight-year-old?
> Me: He is.
> Lawyer: And Sloane is—
> Me: Six.
> Lawyer: You okay?

The part where the judge asked if I wanted a tissue somehow didn't make it into the official transcript. But every other minute detail did—every aside, every little comment from the bench, preserved like scripture.

Maybe the stenographer was too busy crying to hear it.

Then I testified about everything else—essentially this book. Not the family parts, not the private stuff. But the Colorado boys. Jake's first $15,000 investment. The raids. Why I quit. And what I told the IRS.

Lawyer: And this—this is an email from Mr. Schell to you?

Me: Yes.

Lawyer: And the date is April 12th, 2014?

Me: Yes.

Lawyer: The subject line says, "Think about it." Would you just read what the message from Mr. Schell to you was?

Me: "I want you to think about a number to let me buy you out. I think you need to take some time off and maybe work on some less stressful projects. Seriously, think about it and let me know. Jake."

Lawyer: And did you, in fact, let Mr. Schell buy you out?

Me: No. No. I mean—there—I didn't think he was serious..

I was then questioned by my lawyer about the charges—my taxes, my income, the raids and whether I'd lied to a federal agent.

Lawyer: Okay. Did you tell the revenue agents that you were not actively involved in Relief Choices' business operations?

Me: I said I wasn't involved in the day-to-day operations of the business.

Lawyer: Is that true? Were you or were you not?

Me: I was not.

Lawyer: Did you tell the agents in March of 2016 that you were not involved in the operation or management of Relief Choices in any capacity and did not deal with vendors or suppliers?

Me: I did say that I was not involved with the day-to-day operations, and I did state that I wasn't involved with vendors or marijuana—or dealing with the buying and selling.

Lawyer: Okay. Did you ever meet and talk to a vendor?

Me: I mean, yeah, I certainly have met a vendor, but I wasn't coordinating or transacting, I guess, if that's the question.

Lawyer: Further on in Count 1, did you tell the revenue agents on or about August 10, 2016, that you did not own Relief Choices, but only invested in Relief Choices?

Me: Yeah, that statement doesn't make sense. I—I don't...understand how I could be an investor and not an owner, so I don't know—I don't know what that statement means.

Then came the cross examination.

The U.S. attorney—The Robot—fired questions like he was Agent Copenhagen back at my IRS audit, only now the stakes weren't numbers on a page, they were years of my life. He tried to trip me, to catch me contradicting myself. I didn't flinch. By the end, I felt... steady. Maybe even hopeful.

U.S. Attorney: And you know that happened because you were involved in the day-to-day operations of the business, correct?

Me: No.

U.S. Attorney: And you were involved—

Me: No.

U.S. Attorney: —that's how you know the transactions were turned down to begin with, correct?

Me: No. Somebody at the store said the credit card machine doesn't work.

U.S. Attorney: They said it to you.

Me: Or Jake—and Jake said it to me.

U.S. Attorney: And then you help fix it.

Me: Okay.

U.S. Attorney: Credit card transactions are part of the day-to-day operations of Relief Choices.

Me: Okay.

U.S. Attorney: And you were involved in it.

Me: When I met with the agents, they wanted to know who touched the money and who touched the marijuana—that's what they were looking for. That's what they considered day-to-day operations.

Then the ball was volleyed back to my lawyer for re examination

Lawyer: And does the report also indicate that you told the revenue agent at that time that you would have to offset that income because of the raids and things that were damaged or taken, but you cannot get to the items?

Me: I did. I—one thing that was never in any of these government notes or witness notes was the extent of the raids, or... the fact that I said my partner won't call me back, that documents were...still in police custody. With Jake. None of that was ever referenced in any of these, so I did say that—multiple times.

Lawyer: Okay. Did you know about this provision of the Tax Code—this 280E—back when your 2014 tax return was due?

Me: I did not.

Lawyer: Thank you. I have nothing further.

In front of the jury, the Robot dropped his ace: I lived in Bloomfield Hills—a wealthy, manicured suburb. He said it repeatedly like it was proof of my guilt. The subtext was razor sharp: Why did this rich prick think he didn't have to pay his taxes?

The truth? Sarah earns a strong living, and we picked that zip code for one reason: the schools. Nobody in that courtroom saw the wreckage—the millions gone, the financial penalty the government was now demanding so crushing few could pay it in a lifetime. I wasn't fighting to dodge something I owed; I was fighting not to be crushed under something I didn't.

U.S. Attorney: Today you admit you are an owner of Relief Choices, the medical marijuana dispensary on Deckindrey Road, correct?

Me: It's Dequindre. I've always said that. I was proud of it.

U.S. Attorney: Did you say you were proud of it?

Me: Yes, sir.

U.S. Attorney: Okay. So on March 11th, 2016, when you spoke to Revenue Agent Copenhagen and Revenue Agent Linn, you said—

Defense Lawyer: This is beyond the scope of redirect examination, Judge.

The Court: I'm going to allow it. It's all within, as far as I'm concerned, his mindset. Go ahead.

U.S. Attorney: I'm responding to his answer.

The Court: You're responding to his answer?

U.S. Attorney: Yeah, he just said, "I was proud of it."

The Court: Okay.

U.S. Attorney: So on March 11, 2016, when you are interviewed by the IRS regarding your tax returns and your ownership of Relief Choices, you did not tell them you were a 60 percent or a hundred percent owner, did you?

Me: I told them I was an investor and owner of Relief Choices.

U.S. Attorney: Your testimony is you told them you were an owner of Relief Choices; is that correct?

Me: I thought it was pretty clear that I was the owner with them, and, of course, I either said it or it was implied or it was known. I don't—I never doubted that they didn't think I was an owner.

U.S. Attorney: And when you met with them later in August—excuse me, August of 2016—you said, I am the proud owner of Relief Choices and I'm here to tell you about the business that we operate; is that correct?

Me: Well, I wasn't proud around the IRS, but, yes.

U.S. Attorney: But you're proud today?

Me: Yes.

U.S. Attorney: I'm sorry?

Me: I am proud of what I did, correct.

U.S. Attorney: Okay. You're proud to be the owner of Relief Choices?

Me: I'm proud of the patients we served and the community we served.

U.S. Attorney: And you were scared when you spoke to the IRS, was your testimony on direct, correct?

Me: In a way that anybody would be scared, but I was afraid that, you know, I was with the federal government talking about an illegal substance.

U.S. Attorney: And so, because you were scared, instead of saying, I'm the proud owner of Relief Choices, you said, go talk to Jacob Schell, right?

Me: In regards to questions like who handled the cash, where was the marijuana. Mr. Copenhagen was very aggressive during meetings and I just simply didn't have the answers for them. They wanted to know roles, I gave them the role that I played, and I couldn't answer most of their questions and Mr. Copenhagen didn't believe me.

U.S. Attorney: And so you sent them to go talk to Jacob Schell.

Me: I didn't send them to go talk to Jacob Schell. They asked me what Jacob Schell was doing—

U.S. Attorney: No further questions, your Honor.

Most defendants never walk out of a criminal federal trial free—conviction rates hover above 99%. Right before deliberations, my lawyer leaned in and asked, "Would you want to be on a jury going against the IRS?" He didn't have to explain. I understood: ordinary people don't want to draw the attention of one of the most powerful agencies in the federal government. Half the Detroit IRS field office sat in the bleachers throughout the trial, watching like hawks, reminding them what might happen to anyone who crossed the wrong institution.

UNITED STATES OF AMERICA v. RYAN RICHMOND. Or, put another way: "All of us against me."

The feds had scheduled closing arguments for Friday morning — an old playbook move to pressure jurors to reach a verdict quickly.

Jurors spent most of the day in deliberation—a detail my lawyers assured me was a good sign.

At about 4 p.m., Judge Parker sent them a note:

"Do you want to deliberate through the weekend and come back Monday morning?"

I already knew their answer.

Thirty minutes later, they filed back in—faces unreadable, verdict slip in hand.

"On Count One, what does the jury find?"

The jury foreman—an engineer, the same guy I'd asked my lawyers to strike during voir dire—looked down at the slip and read it like he was calling out bingo numbers.

"Not guilty."

For a second, the world made sense again. Holy shit... sanity still exists, I thought. That hope lasted about as long as it takes to inhale.

"Counts Two and Three?"

"Guilty."

The air went heavy.

"Count Four?"

"Not guilty."

A flicker of relief—snuffed out a heartbeat later. Another guilty for good measure.

It was like watching a seesaw where you know exactly how it's going to end—slamming you into the dirt.

Guilty on three of the tax evasion charges. Not guilty on the charge of making false statements to a government official: IRS Agent Copenhagen. They sided with me—and with the Angels—that Jake was my partner. So when I told Copenhagen that Jake handled most of the work and I couldn't answer most of their questions, I wasn't dodging or lying. I was telling the truth. On paper, it wasn't a total loss — but the weight of those guilty counts erased any sense of victory.

One of my lawyers leaned in. "We will appeal."

I was done with them both. Done with hope.

I walked out blank. Sarah and I didn't speak on the ride home. When we got there, her parents were playing with the kids. I just shook my head. That was all it took.

I stayed blank for days.

24

I Couldn't Help My Brother

My brother Chad was two years and 232 days younger than me. He died 4 days after I was arraigned in federal court, awaiting trial in the very federal case that would later incarcerate me. He died at the bottom of a bottle.

With the death, the ICU waiting room, the doctor asking if we wanted to see him one more time, the crematory, the funeral—there was never a clean moment to tell my Richmond side of the family what was going on with me.

So I didn't. I did what Richmond men do—I bottled it up.

For nearly three decades, alcohol ravaged Chad's body—just like it had the generations of Richmond men before him.

Chad was different from me in a thousand ways. But he was also more familiar than I care to admit.

Like the older brothers—and like Gary—did to me, I handed the same treatment down the line. The same little cruelties, the same "toughen up" lessons that are really just pain looking for somewhere to go. I told myself it was normal. That it was brotherhood. It was abuse with a family label on it.

He looked at my dad differently than I did. He was too young to see the cracks—too young to understand how our father could charm a room full of strangers and still go home and not know how to be a caring father, how he could shrink my mother in private in ways no one else ever saw. Chad didn't have my resentment—he had reverence. He wanted approval. He wanted a version of love that wasn't conditional or sharp-edged.

And he wanted to be loved in general—badly—but he never learned how to ask for it. He didn't know how to say what he needed, and when he did try, it came out sideways. Anger. Silence. A shrug. Anything but the truth.

After I left home for the military, he dropped out of school. I knew he needed me, someone. I also knew I needed out. So I chose myself and left him behind, pretending that I would come back for him.

Chad fell into a pattern—bad influences, bad decisions, self inflicted abuse like gravity. No direction. No anchor. He never married. Never had kids. He carried this quiet, grinding confusion like a sentence: never quite knowing where he fit in the world, or if he fit at all.

At the end his stomach had to be drained regularly from the internal swelling. Doctors told him even if he stopped drinking, even a liver transplant wouldn't be enough. It was too late. He took his last sip less than 24 hours before he took his last breath.

I replay that moment more than I care to admit. What could I have done differently? I knew he partied, but I didn't understand fully how far it had gone. Not until I cleaned out his house and found dozens of empty vodka pints—only then did I grasp the extent of his pain.

Only Chad and the party store owner knew how serious his addiction was. And both refused to acknowledge it.

Maybe the whole damn world will wake up and let cannabis sit right next to the cheap plastic vodka bottles Chad used to buy from his "dealer" behind the counter.

Al Capone and my brother taught us one thing: prohibition doesn't work. If only Chad had made different choices. If only, instead of grabbing that vodka bottle, he'd reached for the MK-ULTRA kush on a party store shelf—maybe he'd still be here. If only I had done something different.

I never did come back for Chad. And it still kills me.

The truth is, I don't know if I would've known how—even with the benefit of hindsight. I can replay it now, slow-motion, and still can't find the clean moment where I suddenly become the kind of older brother who knows what to say, what to do, how to reach through all that silence and damage and pull him out.

Chad holding my firstborn child.

25

I'm Going to Prison

I woke before the cell phone alarm on the morning of sentencing, the house still and dark in that pre-dawn way where even the walls seemed to be listening. The kids were still asleep. I let the dog out to relieve herself, standing there in the cold with the door cracked, watching her circle the yard like this was any other morning.

After my morning coffee routine I stared at the built-in, walk-in closet dressers for a long time, feeling that old habit of superstition. I'd learned the hard way that details mattered in courtrooms and cages. Never wear blue or red boxers to anything that might end with handcuffs—colors get you flagged as gang-affiliated, and when intake takes them, you're going commando under your jump suit. So I reached past the red briefs I always liked—that part of my chakra always felt inspired by the color—and grabbed the plain white courthouse ones. I told myself it wasn't fear, just planning. If you can't control the big things, you control what you can. That morning, it was underwear.

I dressed slowly, as if dragging out the minutes might somehow stall the day. White briefs, my newest Hugo Boss suit, crisp white shirt, and the blue tie Sarah had picked—same shade as the party affiliation of my Obama-appointed judge. No second tries; I got it right on the first pass. When I stepped into the bathroom, Sarah was already there, brushing on her makeup, beautiful as ever. She handed me my second cup of coffee and smiled—a steady, brave smile that was harder to look at than anything waiting for me in court.

175

We didn't say much. Not to each other, and not to my in-laws standing in the living room, jackets on, keys in hand, ready to drive our kids to school.

Somewhere along the way, Sarah's parents became the only real parents I'd known in years. They didn't just tolerate me—they stood by me, fully, the way they stood by their own kids.

I kept thinking maybe there was still a version of the day where I walked out with probation, where a reasonable person said something reasonable and the story bent back toward sense. That's the strange part about hope—how it refuses to shut up even when you've given it every reason.

The government wanted eight years.

"We need to make an example of Ryan for the entire marijuana industry," the U.S. Attorney (the Robot) had told the court.

Never mind that I hadn't been inside a dispensary as an owner in a decade.

The downtown Detroit courthouse felt colder than usual — the way government buildings always do when you're desperate for them to feel human. Judge Linda Parker looked down from her perch, her voice calm, almost casual, like she was reading a lunch order.

I really think she saw through the vendetta during the trial. I wasn't sure if she cared.

"Five counts," the clerk announced.

"I have to give you something," she said. "Two years in prison on each count. One year supervised release."

My heart sank, the room was silent and the weight of it all nearly made me collapse in my chair. My stomach caved in. Ten years—that was all I could see. I did the math twice, like maybe the numbers would change if I willed them hard enough. They didn't. The room went distant, sounds muffled, like I was watching my own life from the far end of a tunnel.

Despite already losing nearly $1 million of my own money up until that point, Judge Parker twisted the knife deeper: "Restitution, $2,777,000 — $1.1 million in taxes, $1.67 million in fines."

My two new lawyers (Stu and Hugh) told the judge something that sounded, even to a layman, like basic math: the record showed enough evidence that Jake was my partner. If the government was going to pretend he didn't exist—fine. But they shouldn't be allowed to pin the entire financial loss on me alone. Either prosecute him, or put him on the hook for his share of the restitution.

The U.S. Attorney responded with something so upside-down it didn't even qualify as an argument. He told the court I could always sue Jake for his portion.

Sue him.

As if a civil lawsuit was a substitute for equal justice. As if the government could pick winners and losers, decline to charge the guy standing next to me, then wash their hands and say, Handle it in civil court.

It didn't make sense—legally or in plain English.

The judge bought the government's argument—like they so often do.

"You have a zero percent chance of recidivism," she told me. "You love your family, and they love you. But I still have to… give you some time," she reminded me.

"You'll serve your sentence at a federal prison camp in West Virginia," she said. "Morgantown."

She let the name hang in the air like it meant something I couldn't yet understand. Morgantown. It sounded like a place with football games and tailgates, not somewhere to store the people the country had decided it was done with.

Then she stood and quickly left the bench without another word.

My new lawyer Stu leaned into my shoulder later, outside, when the air hit me and I remembered to breathe. "Concurrent, not consecutive," he said softly. "Two years total, Ryan." You'd think that would have felt like a reprieve. It didn't. All I could think about was my kids—their little lives, still soft and forming—and how my absence would fuck them up in ways I couldn't undo. And then my brain would jump to the other nightmare: the humiliating, surreal reality of showering with other men like it was normal. Two years might as well have been ten in that moment. Both sounded like eternity.

Sarah and I drove home in silence, the two of us pretending not to do the math on birthdays and holidays. The sky was the color of wet cement. Abandoned homes stood guard along the freeway as we drove through Detroit. I watched pot shop and personal injury lawyer billboards fly past and tried to pin meaning to them, past a tired and broken down Detroit, and then a restaurant where I'd once promised to take Sarah.

At the house, we performed the motions of normal. Shoes in the mudroom. Keys in the dish. Lights on in rooms that didn't need them. Grandma and grandpa were playing with the kids. The looks on our faces told them what we already knew–I was going to prison. When the talking in my head got too loud—when the fear of what I was doing to my kids, to my wife, and the unknown world of federal prison started closing in—I'd step out onto the back porch and let myself fall apart. I cried the way you cry when you've held it too long; small at first, then hard and ugly. I kept it quiet so the kids wouldn't hear. It wasn't heroic. It wasn't noble. It was just a man finally accepting the wall he'd run into.

Inside, I hugged them all—too tight, too long. I breathed them in, that mix of shampoo, juice box, and whatever mysterious scent clings to kids who never stop moving. For a moment, I just held on, trying to memorize it.

I thought of my mother, her Lupus, the day she asked me to drive into a neighborhood I didn't belong in, to meet a man I didn't want to meet, just so she could make the pain bearable. That's why I'd gotten into this—not to play outlaw, but to help people like her.

The irony of it sat on my tongue. And, if I'm being honest, I let myself lean into it, maybe too hard—like I was trying to see how far I could push feeling sorry for myself before it tipped into something else.

Self-surrender to prison comes wrapped in this weird, polite paper. No marshals. No Con Air. No black box wrist cuffs. Just a date on a form and instructions that read like hotel check-in: arrive at 11 a.m. It's almost courteous. Almost.

* * *

My genealogy research told me the Richmonds—before Grandpa and Grandma took the hillbilly highway to Michigan—had lived in West Finley, Pennsylvania, right on the West Virginia border. Forty miles from the place I'd now call home.

For seven generations, the Richmonds stayed in those hills.

John Richmond—my Revolutionary War ancestor—settled there after the war, on land he'd been given for his service.

"Frontier Rangers" weren't the powdered-wig kind of soldier. They were the in-between men—militia and scouts who knew the woods, who could move quietly, hunt, track, and fight in terrain that swallowed regular armies. Rifles instead of polished muskets.

Wilderness rules instead of parade-ground rules. The work was ugly: scouting, raiding, protecting settlements, running the edge where "civilization" ended and something older began. "Frontier protection" was the polite phrase. The job mainly involved killing Indians.

There were records that John served in more than one uniform before he became what that headstone claims. Earlier records suggest a connection to serving under George Washington, during the British years, back when Washington was a young officer in the French and Indian War, fighting for the Crown long before he fought against it.

What I do know is this: not much is clear about John Richmond's life before he disappeared into western Pennsylvania. The paper trail and family accounts I've found suggest he was born from a more affluent, early-settler world—Massachusetts and noble British royalty roots. He owned property, and those transactions are in the record—uncommon for a young man back then. More digging points to a family break: John and his brother were raised by a single unwed mother, her petitioning the courts for support from a father described as a wealthy shipping captain moving through Philadelphia ports.

Just like me, he was born out of two different worlds—and in the process, the clean version of his story got erased.

So he did what men like that do. What I did. He escaped. He built a new name out of war, and then out of distance—on what was basically the end of the planet in those days, in the Appalachian hills.

And reading it, I couldn't miss the echo.

Two worlds. A missing origin story. Silence where history should've been. And a man who decided he'd rather start his own story than spend his life begging for someone else's.

* * *

I'd known for months that Monday, June 26th at 11:00 a.m. was the moment I'd have to walk into prison.

Sarah and I kept it to ourselves. We told ourselves the kids were too young to understand. That we could protect them from the countdown. That we could squeeze a few more ordinary months out of life without that shadow hanging over the house. And maybe—if I'm honest—I didn't fully know how to say it. Or I didn't want to.

I finally told them on Friday, three days before check in.

It was one of the hardest things I've ever done. Harder, even, than sitting in a hospice room with a doctor as witness telling my mother we were going to pull the plug while she lay motionless and unconscious. That was awful, but it was clean in a way. Telling your kids you're leaving is something else entirely. It's grief mixed with guilt.

We spent that weekend glued together. At night we all curled up in the same bed. During the day we played like we could outrun Monday if we just stayed busy enough. My older child—my son—kept telling me how much he was going to miss me. He understood more than his little sister did.

And it broke me.

Because there's no way to make it make sense to a child. There's no sentence you can say that turns it into something acceptable. You can try to sound steady, try to sound reassuring, but all they hear is that you're leaving—and the truth is, you are.

* * *

After dinner on Sunday I sobbed as I said goodbye to the kids.

Sarah and I packed the car with little more than what we were wearing and a change of clothes for the morning. Four hundred and twenty miles of silence punctuated by small talk we didn't mean. We stopped for gas once, filling the ride with a podcast about how to survive prison, as if tips from a stranger's voice could prepare me for what was coming.

Mostly, we listened to the tires hum and to the things we couldn't say out loud.

By eleven thirty that night, we rolled into a Marriott on the edge of Morgantown. Beige carpet. Generic art. A convention center that had seen better days. The window looked out over the dark shape of the Appalachians—quiet, still, and indifferent to what was coming.

We didn't talk much. There are only so many ways to say "I'm sorry" when neither of you has anything to apologize for.

We made love like it was the last time, because for a while it would be. Afterward, I lay on my back listening to Sarah breathe, counting seconds between each rise and fall like counting seconds between lightning and thunder. I wondered how she would hold everything together without me and hated myself for the arrogance in that thought. She'd always been stronger than me. The fiction that I was the glue had been comfort more than fact.

Morning came like a verdict. My last free-world meal was Chick-fil-A. A bacon egg and cheese biscuit, hash browns, and a large sized coffee that I nursed like it was bourbon. We sat in the Morgantown FPC parking lot longer than made sense. When it was time, I kissed her. We didn't cry. Not there. I told her I loved her and turned toward the low buildings tucked into the hills.

The oddest thing about walking into federal prison at Morgantown is how ordinary it looks. No razor wire. No towers. No fences at all. Just a campus of dull buildings where the Appalachian fog does the job that barbed wire does elsewhere. The guard at the gate barely looked up. He checked my name against a clipboard, jerked his chin toward R&D—Receiving and Discharge—and went back to not caring.

Intake is humiliation dressed up as procedure. Fingerprints. Mugshot. Strip. Bend. Cough. The same barked commands I'd heard in the county jails, only here they were delivered with the flat boredom of people who were better paid. They handed me brown khakis, socks too small for my size 11 ½ feet, three pairs of underwear thin enough to read through, and flimsy slipper shoes that would be swapped the next day for the same military-style boots I'd been issued years before.

We love telling ourselves we're the land of the free—right up until the moment we start counting cages.

America has about 5% of the world's population and yet locks up roughly a quarter of all the world's prisoners. We're drunk on incarceration and proud of how we hold our liquor. And there I was—one more tally mark on the clipboard—folded into a system that prefers warehousing to healing, punishment to repair, alcohol to cannabis, bodies stacked behind razor wire instead of problems actually solved.

A man with a polo shirt and dead eyes skimmed my file. "Military Police," he said flatly, like he was reading the weather. He looked up. "Don't tell anyone. Cops don't do well here." He let it hang a few seconds, then let the mask drop. "But you know what?" He leaned in until I could smell his coffee and spearmint chewing tobacco. "I don't give a fuck, you piece of fuckin shit." It was so weirdly personal and impersonal at the same time that I almost laughed. Welcome to prison.

No orientation packet. No handshake. Just a wave toward a hallway and the kind of pity you give someone in a hospital gown. A guard shoved a linen bag into my hands with the rest of my issue and pointed toward the dorms. That was the last official help I'd get that day or any other day at Morgantown.

Here's the thing they don't tell you: all prisons are run by inmates. Staff clock in and out. In between, men in khaki feed the place, clean it, fix it, enforce the rules that matter, ignore the ones that don't. The prison is a stage set and the actors are also the crew. You learn the rules by breaking them.

As I wandered into the yard after I arrived—aimless, carrying that fresh-intake disorientation like a scent—another prisoner caught the look on my face. The lost-new-guy look. The where the hell do I go now look. He looked at my paperwork and walked me to my bunk and introduced me to the man I'd be sleeping above. "Wall Street," he said, like the word should come with a trumpet fanfare. He hadn't ever worked a day in his life there. He'd run a payroll and tax return company, mainly to non-profit organizations and "borrowed" three million dollars of their employee's paychecks and corporate funds to leverage a stock options play he was sure couldn't miss. It missed within a week. Ninety percent gone in days. The rest he chased at an Indian casino outside Cleveland, as if doubling down could turn a black hole into a trampoline.

When you steal paychecks from churches, people notice. When you sneer while they notice, judges do too. He'd been sentenced to seventeen and a half years. When I met him, he was almost done. He talked loud and often—like volume could turn bad decisions into war stories. I climbed to the top bunk that first night and told myself I could handle the snoring, the uncleanliness, his bullshit and the way his shoes never quite stayed under his bed. I added a new goal to the list. Survive. Get a new bed.

The first night dragged on like it was daring me to break. If I'm being honest, it was the first time since that first raid almost fifteen years earlier that I actually felt safe—no glancing over my shoulder, no bracing for the sound of boots at the door, no wondering if the day would end in another smashed-in office or home. There was a strange, unsettling calm to it. I stared up at the dimmed ceiling lights, counting sprinkler heads like they were stars, breathing in the stale cocktail of old socks and disinfectant. I thought maybe I'd cry—like that gut-deep release I'd had on the porch back at my real home—but nothing came. Instead, I lay still, listening to men speak in low, coded tones, the kind you use when you're sure someone's listening. And they usually were.

By the end of that first week I'd learned the chow line cadence, the route to the yard, how to find the corner of the track that stayed dry longest after rain. I learned who to avoid in the day room and who controlled the cleaning supplies. I learned that respect is a currency you spend with attitude and posture more than words. And I learned that if a man offers you a seat at his table, you take it, even if you don't plan to sit there tomorrow.

Most of the men I lived with had avoided trial by accepting a plea agreement. The system is built that way: threaten a mountain of time and offer a sliver of hope. Only a very few insisted on rolling the dice in court. I was one of them. We found each other like magnets. We didn't have to talk about the moments when we still ran tape in our heads—what we'd said or what our lawyers could have said or done better. We recognized the way the sting sits under the skin when you believe you were railroaded. The insane idea that serving time might be easier if you'd actually done what they said. There's a particular kind of quiet you carry when you think the story they told about you to the jury wasn't the truth.

One of the first guys to say hello was Justin. He acted like he'd taken a wrong turn out of a Wall Street parking garage and just kept driving until he wound up in Morgantown—clean-cut, educated, the kind of attitude that said he once belonged on trading floors where someone else brought the coffee. He was convicted by a jury after being accused of orchestrating a pump-and-dump stock scheme. The catch? He never dumped. That missing step—the one that makes it a crime—never happened. But in federal court, the story they can sell matters a hell of a lot more than the truth you can prove.

Now he was eating mystery meat under buzzing lights, across from me, talking about markets and Sabbath dinners like both still existed in the same sentence. "The food's not too bad, right?" he said.

I gave him a look that said he'd been down too long.

After that, we ate together most days. It wasn't the kind of friendship built on shared hobbies or geography. He was smart—advanced degrees, the kind of guy who devised investments for big banks. I sold stocks and weed to individuals.

Our bond wasn't built on similarities. It was built on mutual disbelief—and the strange, guilty relief of finally saying your story out loud to someone who just nodded, like he'd lived in your skin.

Everybody needs a job in prison. It's part performance, part utility. One of the inmate doctors—a quiet guy with a past life, doctor children and a revoked medical license—told me I'd be a good fit teaching GED. In the free world if you don't have a high school diploma, no problem. In prison, you enroll or you go to the hole. The guys in class didn't want to be there any more than I wanted to be in West Virginia. I took the job because it kept me out of the dorm, away from Wall Street during most of the day.

Weeks later, I found a different angle. A federally funded program let military veterans inside train service dogs for disabled veterans outside. On paper, it was noble. In practice, like a lot of things that live on federal budgets, it ran on checkboxes and taxpayer wasted grant money.But there was a perk that made it the best program in the compound: dog handlers got their own rooms. Not bunks in open bays—rooms. With doors. One of the highest pay schedules on the compound too: $41 a month. And most important, it got me away from Wall Street.

I pivoted. In short order I wasn't teaching fractions or mitosis; I was teaching a lab mix named Bear to heel. My official duties were one hour on Tuesday mornings. The rest of the time I walked the track and read like I was starving. By the time I left, I had knocked down about one hundred and fifty books—philosophy, psychology, business, religion, biographies, poetry when the days needed smoothing. I stayed out of the TV room except for the Super Bowl and the couple times the Detroit Lions aired in the Pittsburgh market. I didn't gamble. I didn't have a bootlegged cell phone. I didn't owe. I went to bed by nine-thirty, woke up at four-thirty, and made my body into a metronome. It was my way of dulling the edges that cut people who get sloppy.

The library in Morgantown was well-stocked—shelves lined with books mailed in by family members and left behind by doctors, politicians, and men far more educated than me. In the corner sat a small TV and a battered file cabinet of DVDs—every one of them non-violent, G-rated, and safe enough for a Sunday school classroom. One day, after I'd kept myself dry-eyed for weeks out of some dumb pride,

I checked out Field of Dreams. I'd seen it twenty times in the free world. That day, in a plastic chair under fluorescent lights, I cried for a few minutes. Maybe it was the movie, dads and sons and second chances. Maybe it was permission. Maybe it was the loss of my family and kids. Maybe it was feeling sorry for myself again. Sometimes you need a story to give you an alibi for breaking open.

A week later, in that same library, I was deep in a book on Native American history when a guy everyone called Lawyer Bob slid into the seat across from me. He was from Youngstown, once a criminal defense attorney, the kind who took on mobsters and heavyweight drug dealers and actually won. He talked fast and sharp, with the kind of arrogance that only comes from beating the system—until the system turned back on him.

Bob told me how he'd beaten his first federal trial. But the feds don't like losing, and they don't walk away. He said they rewrote the elements of the charge, re-filed the case, and dragged him back into court. This time, they won.

His "crime"? Taking payment from a client. That client had cooked up a fake business and cashed a bogus tax return check, got caught and then used part of the money to pay Bob's legal fees. Bob had no hand in the scheme, no part in the fraud. He just took a check for doing his job. But in America, conspiracy law is like duct tape—stretchy enough to patch anything together. You don't have to do the thing. You just have to stand close enough for them to say you could have.

Now Bob wasn't just convicted; he was on the hook for the whole amount his client had swindled, as if the money he got for his fees had been the same as robbing the Treasury himself. His career gone, his name trashed, his pockets turned inside out. And prison—now his office—became the only place left to practice the law.

Listening to him, I couldn't help but think: conspiracy laws might be the most un-American invention ever dreamed up. Even asset forfeiture at least has the decency to admit it's theft. Conspiracy? That's bullshit. A way to take down whoever's standing too close to the fire, whether they lit the match or not.

Bob invited me to the Lakota sweat lodge—the Inípi.

Because reservations sit on federal land, any jail time from crimes on a reservation lands you in a federal prison. And in that system—on paper, at least—the First Amendment meant they had to allow access to ceremonies: the lodge, the fire pit, the prayers.

So in a place that took our names and gave us numbers, there was still a circle of dirt where we were allowed to be human again—small and honest and hot and quiet.

And I remember thinking, not without a little nausea, that it was probably the same dirt my ancestor John Richmond once stood on—back when men like him called themselves "Frontier Rangers" and built their futures by killing the people who were already there.

After I went through the process of officially changing my religion to Lakota—signing a waiver that I wouldn't sue the BOP for any health issues from the heat or smoke—Bob, me, and four other blood brothers built the fire with care. We crawled into that dome and prayed. We passed the peace pipe. We laughed for five hours every Tuesday after lunch. It was the only place in the compound where tobacco passed legitimately from hand to mouth. Outside the circle, cigarettes were contraband and traded at four bucks a stick. Inside the lodge, the warden handed us tobacco and called it religion.

In a small way, we lived a sliver of what Native people have endured—forced from our homes and then judged for the very thing that brought us peace. The chaplain—the man with the badge and the Bible and, yes, a pair of handcuffs—took a special interest in shutting us down. He was born-again and closeted and angry in a way that made me sad more than mad. He muttered "You boys are not real Indians," like it was an accusation. He filed complaints, changed our schedule without warning and searched for any violation possible. Each time he tried, the First Amendment did what higher powers sometimes can't. Whatever he did always backfired. The only people who disliked him more than the tribe were the other guards. It didn't help his mood that sometimes we drew more men to the lodge than he did to Sunday service.

Even a captive flock knows hypocrisy when it hears it.

The sweat became my clock. I didn't count in days or weeks anymore — I counted in Tuesdays. Every Tuesday in the prison sweat lodge burned into me like a notch on a calendar only I could read.

"Ten more sweats until I go home," I told Bob once. The words sank into my chest with a quiet finality that no date circled on paper ever gave me. Tuesdays became the measure of endurance. A ritual.

I carried that ritual with me when I walked out. At home, I tried to build a sweat lodge in my yard. Bob did the same. But freedom has its own rules. Out there, it wasn't the chaplain or the guards who held authority. It was our wives.

* * *

My neighbors in the dorm were a cross-section of America's failures — blue-collar, white-collar, and no-collar at all. On one side of my room was a man eighteen years into a thirty-year sentence for some white-collar scheme none of us could fully make sense of. He said he'd worked with Bernie Madoff. Maybe he had.

I didn't push. That was an unwritten rule in prison: you don't ask about a man's crime unless he offers it up himself. Stories are currency, and some guys spend theirs freely. Others hoard them like commissary snacks.

To my left, a polite kid from Indianapolis who'd "borrowed" from his employer's bank account to chase parlays on sports apps. He told me FanDuel paid better than DraftKings and if he'd stuck to one, he might not have gotten caught. He said it like he'd learned a rule he planned to use later. I hoped he was kidding. I bet he was.

You'd think I would've clicked with the white-collar guys, the men who wore the same shirts I used to wear and talked about cash value life insurance policies like it was Monday Night Football. I didn't. A lot of them took a plea and floated on a cloud of I'm-not-like-these-guys. Some were decent. Some were slimeballs with good vocabularies. Most pretended their crimes were refined, a matter of paperwork and misunderstanding, not desire and nerve.I found myself walking and talking more often with the guys who moved bricks of cocaine and heroin—mostly Black men who'd been "down" before and would probably be "down" again. They didn't pretend. They understood the game. At Morgantown—and in most prisons—half the compound seemed to be there on drug cases.

Recidivism is highest with drug offenses, especially when guys went right back to dealing. "Recidivism" is just a bureaucratic word for the loop: do your time, get out, and end up right back in. And at Morgantown that loop was more common than not.

A lot of the men I talked to had already done a bid or two. Some liked Morgantown so much they tried to land back there as part of their plea. They knew the guards by name and the guards knew them. Prison wasn't some life-changing punishment. It was a reset button. A place to regroup. A few of them said it felt like coming home.

Inside, the guards had a running joke: "We'll leave the light on for you."

I didn't agree with what some of these men sold—especially the fentanyl guys. Fentanyl took two people I loved, too early. But I was in no position to sit on a high horse. If I liked someone, I liked them. I wasn't trying to convert anyone. I was doing the same time they were doing.

I'd talk about the hypocrisy out loud. The professionals I knew outside—mostly lawyers—who did cocaine on weekends and still slept in their own beds at night, not on the steel cots we lived on. I'd say it plain: people have the right to put whatever they want in their bodies.

The people I kept my distance from weren't always the bad kind of drug dealers. It was the scammers—the guys who made a living off the vulnerable. That felt colder to me than selling a vice to someone who came looking for it.

The more time I did, the clearer it became: if you want to fix prison, you don't start with prison. You fix the war that fills it.

Johann Hari wrote it plain in Chasing the Scream, a book that made the rounds inside. End the war on drugs and you fix society. You fix families. You fix futures. But that solution doesn't feed the machine. The prison-and-court business runs on the bodies of the addicted and the poor—and at Morgantown, the ambitious.

I became friends with some of those ambitious guys, the ones who told the truth about losing everything and expecting nothing back. The ones who never concerned themselves with being legitimate. Their honesty was raw and unpolished—more believable than the boardroom regret the white-collar guys rehearsed for their sentencing judges.

And it wasn't lost on me that I belonged at both tables.

I was a drug dealer too—just one with a collared shirt and a lobbyist's phone number stored in my cell phone.

Different packaging. Same system.

* * *

Prison is a slow, grinding education in small humiliations and forced compliance. The laundry never actually smelled clean—just a little less not-clean. By the end of the first month, I'd ditched every piece of government-issued clothing, except khaki uniforms, for hand-me-down shoes and fresh items from the commissary. I learned which guards would let you walk by with a shred of dignity and which ones made it their goal to strip it away. Eventually, I learned the safest move was to ignore them all—because the truth is, they were all serving a longer sentence than any of us. There are a hundred little tricks to staying invisible in prison, and every one of them starts with not inviting attention.

Less than a week after I arrived at Morgantown, Justin and I fell into a routine. We'd meet for chow, then drift to the law library for hypothetical debates—like two guys killing time at an airport bar.

We talked markets, politics, philosophy. He was a left-wing Democrat. I was "apolitical," which mostly meant I didn't trust anyone enough to join their team. But to keep it fun, I'd take the right-wing side half the time—not because I believed it, but because a debate with no resistance is just a lecture. Justin didn't lecture. He engaged. And I liked that.

I enjoyed those conversations more than I expected to. I always learned something—sometimes about the world, sometimes about myself. Being around him made me a nicer person, which is not a small thing in a place designed to break you down.

Unless you asked the Justice Department, Justin was the smartest-dumbest, most sincere, most unwittingly innocent man I'd met in a long time. He wasn't like most of the guys on the compound. He still talked like the world was rational. Like truth mattered. Like people could be persuaded.

In prison, that kind of innocence stands out. And Justin had been targeted by a few of the guards in West Virginia—one of them had even spit, "You dirty Jew."

Every system invents its own process. In prison, it was chow times, count times, and the sudden storms of shakedowns by the cops—as we often referred to them. The higher-up prisons had titles like Boss or Boss Man. We passed the days by gossiping about which guard was now sleeping with the small minority of female guards, which guard was about to transfer, and how the approval of Ozempic in the federal health care system literally lightened the load overnight. And the guards did the same–gossiping about us. Our lives were intertwined like any workplace situation. Gossip moved faster than commissary lines. Stories were traded like Mac's the prison currency.

Most prisons ran on stamps, but Morgantown was different.

Here, the economy was based on mackerel. Vacuum-sealed pouches of fish — "macs" — ruled everything. One mac was worth a buck even though it cost $1.40 at commissary. That extra forty cents? Just baked-in inflation. In prison and outside, the free market wasn't free.

Macs bought everything. Haircuts or a slice of dorm-made pizza grilled on an iron: 5 macs. Four macs got you a single Newport, or a few hands at the poker table. Macs were harder to count than stamps, but more durable than Ramen, and unlike cash — which was contraband — they were perfectly legal. Technically.

In Morgantown, the whole system ran on them. Supply, demand, hustle. The same economic forces as the outside world — just fishier.

You couldn't eat dollar bills. But macs? They spent, they traded, and worst case — they fed you.

* * *

The hardest part of prison wasn't the noise, Wall Street, the boredom, or the way time turns into cement. It was knowing my kids were out there in the world without their dad—having to explain it to friends, or dodge the question altogether.

"Where's your dad?"

I missed everything. The ordinary moments. The piggy back rides. Hide and seek. Homework. The stuff you don't think you'll miss until it's gone. And I couldn't stop thinking the same thought, over and over: How bad is this going to fuck them up later? That was the one thing that brought me real anger inside. Not the system. Not the case. Me.

It wasn't just me who got institutionalized. My kids did too.

Sarah made the 420-mile drive at least once a month, about ten trips total. The kids learned the routine: the pat-downs, the bag checks, the sign-in clipboard at security—like one of them might suddenly decide to smuggle contraband for their father. They saw the razor wire out the visiting-room window, the lines that secured the SHU. You might know it as the hole.

Phone calls weren't much better.

Every five minutes, that cold, disembodied voice cut into our conversation like a knife:

"This call is from a federal prison."

For them, it became routine. A cue to pass the phone from one small hand to the next.

Sarah and the kids would send letters, and sometimes—when the prison mail gods allowed—they actually made it to me. They carried more than words. They smelled of home, of the life I'd stepped out of but could still reach through words on paper and my daughter's amazing drawings.

I had ten minutes a day to call. Split evenly, that was five minutes per kid. On some days, I had time to talk to my wife, filling me in with stories from the house—breakfast-table debates, report cards, new shoes. The little things that felt like everything.

She'd tell me how the dog still slept on my side of the bed. Guarding the spot, like she was still waiting for me to come home.

What she didn't tell me was how bad it really was—raising the kids alone, juggling PTA, birthday parties, and the endless shuttle runs in every direction, all while working full time and trying to keep the whole thing from tipping over.

What I didn't tell her was what happened on my end: the man at intake who looked right through me and called me a piece of shit. Wall Street. The chaplain. The little humiliations that stacked up so fast you stopped counting.

Even if I'd wanted to unload it, there wasn't room. Calls were short, visits were crowded, and life was always happening on both sides of the glass. So we made a deal without ever saying it out loud—each of us would carry the worst parts alone, so the other didn't have to.

Not everyone had someone waiting for them on the outside.

A lot of the guys had been down so long, their families gave up. Some had stopped writing. Others stopped caring. Eventually, so did the inmates.

Wall Street was one of them.

He was due to be released after thirteen years down, but prison was the only world he knew anymore. Over time, he'd replaced whatever family he had with a few guards who pretended to listen and a handful of inmates who were too polite to end his one-way conversations.

I actually felt sorry for him.

When his release date came, he did what I always suspected he would. He picked a fight with a Black inmate—called him a "nigger," and maybe even worse, a "primitive." Right out of the Warren Police Department's playbook.

They sent him to the hole. But even that wasn't enough to keep him locked up. Wall Street had pulled this act too many times. The staff had enough. He wasn't ready for the outside world—but they were done with him inside. He overstayed his sentence by a few months and got shipped to a halfway house with his official address listed as the nearest homeless shelter.

Prison can take everything from you—even the idea of freedom.

Wall Street reminded me of Brooks Hatlen from The Shawshank Redemption—an old man institutionalized beyond repair. Brooks tried to kill a fellow inmate just to avoid leaving. Wall Street didn't have that kind of guts, but his fear ran just as deep.

* * *

The chaplain tried one more time to shut down the sweat lodge just before I left, citing some made-up "security concern" about indecent exposure after leaving our shirts off for too long exiting the Inipi, and the threat of men who didn't practice things the way he thought they should. It got tossed again. We walked past him on the yard later and he muttered his line about any of us being "real Indians." I almost thanked him. The First Amendment held, even in a place built to remind you of all the rights you'd temporarily lost. Sometimes that's what freedom looks like in America—men with pale skin and prison-issue pants sitting in a circle of dirt, passing a pipe, praying for people they love on the outside.

I'd gone in thinking prison would be all punishment, no grace. And a lot of days, that's exactly what it was. But every so often, grace found a side door, slid onto the metal bench beside you at six in the morning while you ate stale cereal with milk that had gone sour. Sometimes it wore fur—a dog's head heavy in your lap. Sometimes it had ink—swastikas curling across a man's skull while he told you the truth about what he'd done, and then asked for the truth about what you hadn't. Sometimes it sounded like a pipe tapping gently against stone as you crawled out of the sweat lodge into bright cold air, small and clean for just a minute.

Morgantown wasn't a prison in the way people imagine it. And it didn't have open bay showers either if you were still wondering. It was fog curling over an Appalachian campus. It was the way men rebuilt themselves when no one was watching. It was bankers and scammers and guys who moved weight across lines drawn by other men. It was me. And it took everything that didn't matter and stripped it away, leaving a small pile that did—my wife's leg brushing against mine in the dark, my kids' hair under my chin, the heat inside the lodge, the thud of my shoes on the dusty track, and the slow turning of pages in books I'd never made time for before.

Two years wasn't ten. And with the congressional reforms that had passed a few years earlier—the First Step and Second Chance Acts—rewarded guys who stayed out of trouble—I wasn't going to serve two. I was only going to serve one.

But some nights, they felt like the same number.

When the day finally came and I could say, "No more sweats," I stood for that last headcount and thought:

I will never voluntarily drive myself to prison again.

Will I miss it? I thought about Judge Parker saying "Morgantown" like it was summer camp. I thought about the intake officer's tobacco-stained smirk and dead eyes. I thought about Wall Street's endless voice, Justin's steady calm, and Bob's jokes in the steam. And I knew the answer.

We tell stories to make sense of the parts that don't line up. Here's mine.

I went to prison at a place without a fence. I checked in like a guest at a motel you couldn't leave. I was told to keep quiet about the military cop I used to be. I slept above a man who stole paychecks and under a ceiling that sometimes felt an inch from my face. I taught men to pass a test and a dog to sit. I walked the track in endless circles and read my way into a smaller, sharper honesty. I prayed in a dome, pissed off a chaplain, and counted Tuesdays like stepping stones across a river.

I made friends with a guy who never dumped and with men who'd moved bricks. I learned my country—the one I love, the one I served for six years—locks up a quarter of the world's prisoners and calls it justice. I learned grace can be cheap and priceless at the same time.

I was a white-collar drug dealer who thought legitimacy would protect me. The war on drugs found a new target: legitimacy. I traded one set of rules for another, swapped one badge for a number stitched on my chest.

 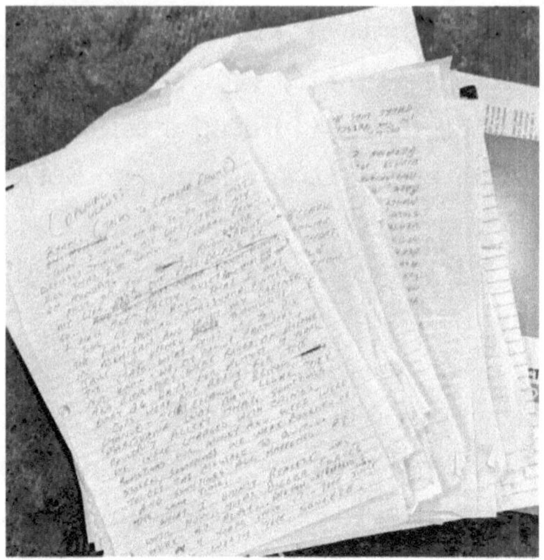

The only photo of me in federal prison, alongside copies of the handwritten manuscript that eventually became this book.

The Mac (prison currency)

26

Halfway Home

On the day of my release, Morgantown was in the middle of a hunger strike—something I'd only heard about from friends who spent time at higher up institutions, and never imagined I'd be part of. Hunger strikes are the nuclear option for prisoners: the last resort to draw attention to grievances and force the hand of those in power.

This one had a clear trigger—a portion of the already bloated staff was being transferred to nearby Misery Mountain, one of the bloodiest prisons in America. It was home to the worst of the worst—men serving life, predators with nothing left to lose. The kind of place where guards wore stab vests just to hand out lunch trays, and where "being an asshole" wasn't a management style anymore—it was a survival liability. They weren't happy about the move, and because they couldn't take it out on the Bureau of Prisons, they took it out on us. Every fan in every dorm disappeared during a week when the heat index pushed 100.

I joined the strike for two reasons. First, I'd already been trying to detox from the expired meat and the high-sodium commissary sludge. Second, in prison, you either fall in line or you stand out—and standing out can get you hurt.

What they didn't know was I already had my own system. Every month, I fasted to purge my body. So a few skipped meals wasn't going to kill me.

When my name was called that morning to report to R&D, I was already packed. The admin building buzzed with talk of pepper-ball guns and "heavy response" to the protest—fake cops playing soldier against middle-aged men in a minimum-security camp. Nothing like the response that would've unfolded at Misery Mountain.

I'd escaped just in time, but I left with hunger strike stamped onto the short list of things I never thought I'd do. It wasn't a badge I wanted—just proof that the place could still push you far enough to surprise yourself.

I'd stood with men who challenged authority—men who refused to pretend the rules made sense just because someone with a badge or a clipboard said they did. Rules handed down like weather. Arbitrary. Unappealable. Designed less to correct you than to remind you who owned the air.

I didn't come out of it romanticizing rebellion. I came out understanding it.

Outprocessing was quick—and very satisfying. They slid me a stack of printed, MapQuest-style directions, like the internet hadn't moved past dial-up, and told me I had six hours to get to the Detroit halfway house. Google said the drive was five and a half. That left me thirty minutes for wrong turns, bad traffic, or... other extracurriculars.

Before I went to Morgantown, I'd already mapped it out in my head: when I got out, I'd stop by the original Richmond burial plot in West Finley, Pennsylvania. I'd say hello to a family I somehow knew better than the family I grew up around, the ones now who kept their distance from me. I told myself that standing on their ground—seeing where they lived, where they ended—might wake something up in me I'd been missing for years.

But the rules said I couldn't.

When I stepped outside, I carried it all—the heat of the lodge still clinging to my skin, the quiet of the morning track, the feel of cheap commissary greys against my legs. And, just like the day I came in,

Sarah was there at the door. Same road home, only in reverse—more to say now, and even more we didn't need to.

* * *

A halfway house is supposed to be a bridge—structured, supervised, a soft landing after prison. Curfews, check-ins, maybe a little job support. On paper, it's meant to help you get your feet under you again. A safer place to fail forward.

That's where I was headed.

Detroit. The very city I'd refused to open a dispensary in—too unstable, too dangerous—was now home. I had no say in it.

The building sat deep behind enemy lines—past 8 Mile, across a border we'd carefully avoided for years. This wasn't the new downtown with high-end lofts and hipster coffee. This was the part of Detroit that even Detroiters call the bad part. Bombed-out houses, burned-down churches, and corner stores with bars on every window.

It felt less like a bridge and more like a test: Welcome back. Let's see if you can survive this.

Not that I needed a "transition," but I was grateful to spend the last stretch of my sentence closer to Sarah and the kids. What I didn't know was that, unlike the prison camp I came from, the halfway house was a mixing bowl of inmates from everywhere—Misery Mountain included. Violent offenders. Child molesters. Hardened addicts. I'd never grasped how rampant drug use was in other prisons until I landed there. Inside, you're drug-tested often—but only for what they expect to find. The worst highs? They glide right under the radar.

One was spice, or K2—the same synthetic cannabinoid the State of Michigan once accused me of manufacturing. The other was roach spray, known on the cell blocks as "KD," "Wasp Dope," or "Katie." The recipe was as crude as it was effective: soak a sheet of paper or cardboard in the stuff, let it dry, light a corner, and inhale the toxic fumes.

The effect was anything but crude.

Some users freeze where they stand, eyes vacant, bodies locked up like mannequins. Others stagger around like extras from a zombie flick—erratic, unpredictable, dangerous. And because it doesn't show up on a standard prison 10-panel drug test, it's the perfect poison.

In Morgantown, we'd had a few guys who were regular connoisseurs of roach-spray. One guy barked at the guards like a pit bull all the way to the hole.

But my favorite was Mater. Give him a hit and a little space, and he'd air guitar for hours. We'd yell "Play Free Bird!" from across the dorm, and damned if he didn't play every solo note for note.

It was funny—until it wasn't. One night around midnight, I woke to see him belly-down, "swimming" across the bathroom floor, screaming at the top of his lungs. By morning, he was gone—shipped to a higher-security joint. Probably for the best. A place where he could score safer dope and where the guards would care even less.

At the halfway house, the staff pretended not to notice the constant cigarette smoke and roach-spray haze in the bathroom, or the zombies drifting through the halls. Their only real line was: "Get back to your room."

I'd shower and walk out technically cleaner, but carrying the sweet, stale mix of Newports and Raid. I couldn't wait to get out. The only ticket was work—so I took it. Twelve-hour days, six days a week. The Hemp Well warehouse became my three-quarter home. Work never felt so satisfying before in my life.

It turned into a second home. Sarah and the kids would show up after school with dinner, games—and sometimes the dog—once their day was finally done. For a few hours each night, we could be a halfway family.

I even got an unexpected reunion at the halfway house.

Hansberry was there—the shady drug cop who'd zip-tied my staff, the same guy who later caught a sentence of his own. We ended up under the same roof at the Detroit halfway house, passing each other in the hallway like two men who'd taken different routes to the same dead end.

He tossed me a fist bump and started flexing, bragging about knocking over dealers—the same story he'd tell again and again in the halfway house. Easy scores. No shame. He talked about it like it was a credential, like something you'd put on a résumé.

Then I told him who I was.

I walked him through our dispensary's location, asked about his task force's CIA connection—and, most of all, about his old boss, "Dutch." Everything in him tightened. The grin died. He didn't argue. Didn't posture. He went cold. He just stared at the floor like the tiles might answer for him. And that's when I saw it: fear. Not of some cartel that never forgets being robbed. Not of the retribution he'd earned. But of the question itself.

My breaking point at the halfway house came over something small—but it didn't feel small. Two pairs of my sweatpants, a pair of jeans and a lone T-shirt vanished from the dryer. Most of the guys there truly needed the transition, and I didn't mind helping someone who was genuinely short on basics. But when it's your own housemates stealing from you, you realize the lesson's over—and it's time to move on.

Almost on cue, my counselor told me I'd been approved for home confinement—an arrangement that meant I could live with Sarah and the kids, go to work, and come straight home. That was the whole bargain. A GPS tether clamped around my ankle, reporting my location every second. They didn't need guards anymore. They had a satellite.

I wasn't about to risk that thin strip of freedom by getting cute with their rules.

But even "good news" came with a leash. The message underneath it was the same one I'd been hearing since the first set of cuffs: comply, or we decide your world gets smaller. Moving back to Detroit wasn't an option. If I pushed, if I argued, if I violated and tried to live like a normal person, they could send me right back—Detroit, or worse, West Virginia.

So once again I did what this system trains you to do: I nodded, I adjusted, I conformed—because the alternative wasn't freedom. It was punishment.

27

Court, Again

On my son's tenth birthday—my appellate lawyer, Stu—the same guy who'd handled some of my state appeals and once called me Al Capone, like I was some modern rerun of the old story: they couldn't get him for bootlegging, so they sent the IRS—filed a petition for a writ of certiorari, formally asking the United States Supreme Court to take my case.

A few months earlier, we'd been shut down at the Sixth Circuit Court of Appeals after arguing something no court had truly confronted before: that using § 280E not just to tax someone, but to put them in a cage, is unconstitutional.

I am the only person in American history who has been sent to prison because of that provision in the tax code. The Sixth Circuit felt the weight of that fact and basically shrugged it upstairs, suggesting: "This is a question for the Supreme Court."

I wasn't the only one knocking on that door. Another case, cleaner and more traditional, was already climbing the same staircase: Canna Provisions et al. v. Bondi. Their lawsuit goes right at the heart of § 280E—how it guts cannabis dispensaries by denying ordinary deductions like rent, payroll, and basic operating costs—and, just as importantly, how that same mechanism could be used to send people to prison. The appeals court in their case dismissed them with a legal Catch-22: "You cannot state a claim that has not happened. None of you have been sent to prison."

Well, I have.

That single detail tied their case to mine like a chain. Their legal roster reads like a Legal Hall of Fame plaque: David Boies, the lawyer who helped win marriage equality at the Supreme Court, who argued the government's side in the Microsoft antitrust case, and who has been in the middle of more landmark battles than most lawyers will ever read about. They have funding. They have structure. They have the kind of institutional respect I've never had and probably never will.

My hope was simple and impossible at the same time: that one or both of our cases would get heard. The Supreme Court doesn't take many cases; when it does, it's usually because the question won't go away on its own. Cannabis isn't a fringe issue anymore—it's baked into everyday American life. Just like the No Pot Shops founder Mr. Schuette had predicted, In a lot of towns, you can count more dispensaries than Starbucks, yet those same businesses are barred from deducting the basic costs of staying open. The lawyers who live in that world believed the Justices might finally be ready to confront § 280E head-on.

I wanted to see that same system—the one that built careers and padded budgets on the backs of cannabis users, the one that raided my home and shredded my family—forced to offer something like redemption.

And then, on November 17th, the Supreme Court of the United States denied my petition. No reason, no oral argument, no written explanation. Just a line on their website:

Petition DENIED.

All caps, like a digital shout. A reminder that my case, my family, the insanity of weed being considered more dangerous than fentanyl, my time in prison—all of it—does not rise to the level of their concern. No further comment. Nothing to see here. Move on.

A week later, the other case arrived at the same dead end. Different plaintiffs, different polish, different pedigree—and the same silent dismissal. It wasn't even personal. That was the worst part. The door didn't slam. It didn't creak open. It simply never moved.

We don't want to hear it.

Then—one week later—President Donald Trump did something no president had done: he said out loud what millions of Americans already knew, acknowledging cannabis's medical value and ordering federal agencies to begin moving marijuana out of the government's most dangerous category and toward Schedule III.

On paper, it sounded like progress. Like the country finally admitting what families already knew. Like my mother's relief mattered more than some bureaucracy's fear. Like an overdue nod to the countless patients Jake and I helped back when helping people was still treated like an organized crime problem.

But executive orders don't erase the past. They don't refund the years. They don't un-raid a home or erase a child's memory of visiting dad in federal prison.

And the order didn't suddenly make cannabis "safe" in the eyes of the culture. It didn't change the social message that has been pumped into Americans for a century: Alcohol is legal because it's culturally entrenched—not because it's harmless. Cannabis was criminalized because it was politically useful—not because it was uniquely dangerous.

Law followed power, not science.

It didn't change what happened to people like my brother. It didn't fix what happened to me.

What it did do was expose the lie at the center of it all. It was power, finally speaking plainly—calling the absurdity what it was.

If cannabis has medical value—real legitimacy—then the old story collapses. The story they used to justify the raids. The story they used to justify the sentences. The story that turned a plant into a weapon of mass destruction—and turned my life into a cautionary tale.

28

The Journey

My whole life, I chased legitimacy.

Legitimacy in my family roots. Legitimacy so I could look like the other kids at school. Legitimacy so I wouldn't end up poor like the generations before me. Legitimacy in business—doing it clean, by the book.

And what I learned was this: to hell with legitimacy.

It's a made-up word—mostly used by people who want to be accepted by people they've decided are better than them. It's approval dressed up as virtue. A hunger for permission.

The legitimacy crowd doesn't start a baseball card business before puberty. They don't ask a colonel to let them leave early. They don't start a commercial real estate firm before 30. They don't open the state's first licensed dispensary. They don't defy a prison chaplain. They don't fight back inside a system designed to make sure you lose.

My whole life I'd been different. And eventually I learned to see the legitimacy in that.

Because it's always more fun to be a pioneer than a settler.

My entire life, I worried about what other people thought of me—how I looked. Not just in a room, in the flesh, but on paper.

My business career was built on doing the right thing and making the right headlines. My LinkedIn stayed polished and current, bragging about the latest deal, the next conquest, the next proof that I belonged in the room. Even during the raids—when my name got dragged through the papers—it mattered more to me to set the record straight than to sit still and feel what was happening.

And after I was convicted—after a federal felony stamped itself onto my record like a brand—I doubled down. I got louder. More defensive. More obsessed with controlling the story.

I wasn't exactly telling the whole truth when I dedicated this book to my children "so they could understand when they were old enough."

In some part I started out writing it for you—so you could understand why, what, where, when, and how my life ended up where it did. So you could see it wasn't all my fault. That I wasn't the villain in my own story.

But something changed while putting words to paper.

I don't care what you think anymore.

I wear these scars like a badge. I care more about the journey than the approval. The breadcrumbs I left along the way matter more than the verdict strangers reach at the end.

To hell with legitimacy.

* * *

Prison gave me something I hadn't touched in years: time. Time to think. Time to disconnect. Time to heal. Time to see, with absolute clarity, just how much my family meant to me.

I worked out. I read nearly 150 books. I wrote most of what you're reading now.

Maybe the best gift prison gave me was the silence in my head. For the first time in nearly fifteen years, the fear that stalked me daily went quiet. No driveway to pull into, no office door to approach—so the PTSD stayed buried.

Now that I'm out, it's creeping back.

Every time I roll into my driveway or park outside my office, my chest tightens. The old reflex flares—raids, sirens, boots kicking in the door. My brain runs the same loop: They're here.

Years have passed, but the wiring never reset. The shock still crouches in the corners of ordinary moments. And I'm okay with that. It's part of the journey—collateral damage.

The single greatest thing I did in West Virginia was learn to forgive.

I forgave the people you've met in these pages—the ones who abused power, who turned their backs on me, who raided my home, who could've been better parents, who stole from me, shut down my sweat lodge, lied under oath, and threatened my family.

And I forgave myself—both for the man I thought I could be, and for the man I actually am.

Because holding on to all of it was killing me.

Letting go was how I took my power back.

Prison is full of tough guys. Full of anger. But I learned that real toughness isn't about rage—it's about forgiveness. Real forgiveness. Braver, even, than opening the first medical marijuana dispensary in a state still drunk on prohibition.

Acknowledgement

A special thanks to my wife and children for their enduring support. To my editor, Ronit Wagman—my only shrink—who pushed me to put Ryan onto the page. And to my high school creative writing teacher, Mrs. Doty, *Jeremy's mom.*

Afterword

I didn't write this book to relitigate my case or to ask for sympathy. The courts exist for that. What I wanted was a record—of how it felt to build something in good faith while the law shifted under our feet, and of what happens when the system decides you'll be the example.

Legalization didn't arrive cleanly. It came in layers: ballot language, loopholes, new rules, old instincts. People like me tried to operate inside the gray, believing that transparency and compliance would count for something. Sometimes they did. Sometimes the moment you became visible, you became useful—as a warning label.

I've spent years thinking about responsibility—where mine begins, where it ends, and where the system's failures take over. I made decisions. I own them. But accountability is supposed to run both ways. When the law changes and enforcement refuses to, when policy evolves but punishment stays frozen in time, the message is simple: the truth doesn't matter as much as the outcome.

This book isn't an argument against the rule of law. It's an argument for coherence—for laws that reflect reality, for enforcement that matches intent, and for a system capable of admitting when it got something wrong. If redemption is real, it starts with honesty: honest about what happened, honest about who benefited, honest about who paid.

I'm still living in the aftermath. Appeals remain pending. New questions have been raised by the rescheduling of cannabis. And I have asked the President of the United States for a pardon. I don't know how any of it will end.

For now, I wait.

*The Only American Sent
to Prison for the Pot Tax*

HIGH TIMES

Excerpt from a March 2026 High Times article

In my reflections, I keep coming back to the same uncomfortable truth: cannabis legalization didn't end the war. It rebranded it. Our culture has shifted, but the system won't. Some day it will need to shift again—because the machine never stops, it just changes uniforms and letterhead.

People love to talk about this era as if it were inevitable—like legalization was a smooth march forward led by wise policymakers. It wasn't. It was messy. It was bloody. It was human. It was expensive.

And for some of us, it was a cage.

About The Author

Ryan Richmond is a serial entrepreneur and an early pioneer in Michigan's medical marijuana industry. His path has collided with state and federal enforcement, media attention, and the shifting politics of cannabis legalization. Today, he's focused on rebuilding—family first—and on telling the truth about what happened. He lives in Bloomfield Hills, Michigan, with his family.